SCIENCE FOUNDATIONS

Planetary Motion

SCIENCE FOUNDATIONS

SCIENCE
FOUNDATIONS

Planetary Motion

P. ANDREW KARAM AND BEN P. STEIN

Planetary Motion

Chelsea House
An imprint of Infobase Publishing
132 West 31st Street
New York NY 10001

Library of Congress Cataloging-in-Publication Data
Karam, P. Andrew.
 Planetary motion / by P. Andrew Karam and Ben P. Stein.
     p. cm. — (Science foundation)
 Includes bibliographical references and index.
 ISBN 978-1-60413-017-1 (hardcover)
 1. Planetary theory. 2. Planets. 3. Galaxies. 4. Celestial mechanics. I. Stein, Ben P. II. Title. III. Series.
 QB361.K37 2009
 523.4—dc22
                    2009002040

Chelsea House books are available at special discounts when purchased in bulk quantities for businesses, associations, institutions, or sales promotions. Please call our Special Sales Department in New York at (212) 967-8800 or (800) 322-8755.

You can find Chelsea House on the World Wide Web at
http://www.chelseahouse.com

Text design by Kerry Casey
Cover design by Ben Peterson
Composition by EJB Publishing Services
Cover printed by Bang Printing, Brainerd, MN
Book printed and bound by Bang Printing, Brainerd, MN
Date printed: August, 2010
Printed in the United States of America

10 9 8 7 6 5 4 3 2

This book is printed on acid-free paper.

All links and Web addresses were checked and verified to be correct at the time of publication. Because of the dynamic nature of the Web, some addresses and links may have changed since publication and may no longer be valid.

Contents

A Billion-Mile
Hole-in-One

8*:54 P.M., June 30, 2004.* Mission control center, 13 miles northeast of Hollywood, inside the Jet Propulsion Laboratory in Pasadena, California. Scientists and engineers nervously watch their instruments. It has been nearly an hour and a half. The *Cassini* spacecraft should have fired its engines to enter **orbit** around Saturn. During those 90 minutes, radio signals from the spacecraft sped across the **solar system** to bring the news to Earth. If the engines burned their way into Saturn's orbit, it would be the latest achievement for a spacecraft that had been in space for almost seven years. If the burn was successful, it would be a triumph for the engineers who had built the craft and for the scientists who had planned *Cassini's* path to the outer solar system.

Cassini blasted off from Earth on October 15, 1997. It rode atop one of the world's most powerful launch rockets, the *Titan IVB/Centaur*. Weighing over 12,000 pounds (or over 5,500 kilograms) and standing more than 20 feet (6 meters, or m) tall, *Cassini* was far too large to be launched directly from Earth to Saturn. Instead, it took a scenic route, swinging past Venus, the Earth, and Jupiter. *Cassini* did not take this route to get a lot of pretty pictures. The planets' **gravity** fields yanked *Cassini* toward them, speeding up the spacecraft so it could travel quickly into the outer solar system. Each of these

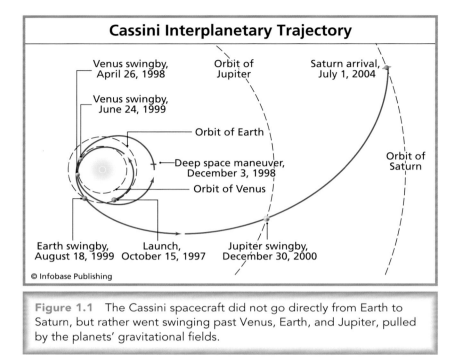

Cassini Interplanetary Trajectory

Venus swingby,
April 26, 1998

Venus swingby,
June 24, 1999

Orbit of Jupiter

Saturn arrival,
July 1, 2004

Orbit of Earth

Deep space maneuver,
December 3, 1998

Orbit of Saturn

Orbit of Venus

Earth swingby,
August 18, 1999

Launch,
October 15, 1997

Jupiter swingby,
December 30, 2000

© Infobase Publishing

Figure 1.1 The Cassini spacecraft did not go directly from Earth to Saturn, but rather went swinging past Venus, Earth, and Jupiter, pulled by the planets' gravitational fields.

gravity-assist maneuvers was risky—*Cassini* actually came frighteningly close to the Earth, passing only 727 miles (1,170 kilometers, or km) from the **planet** in a planned maneuver to pick up even more speed. All of this maneuvering, all of the worry, was simply to take advantage of the geography of the solar system to help get a big spacecraft to the outer solar system in the shortest time possible— and to get as many scientific instruments as possible to a remote but beautiful and fascinating place. What made it all possible was a smart and dedicated group of scientists and engineers, a lot of fast computers, and a detailed understanding of planetary motions.

How did humankind ever learn to send a spacecraft to another planet in the solar system? It all started thousands of years ago, when people could not even get off the ground. Men and women looked in amazement at the night sky. They wondered what the stars were and why they moved the way they did. They saw that some stars stayed fixed next to each other. Yet other points of light moved from day to day about the sky. From there, early **astronomers** realized that some of those lights were not stars at all, but instead objects that were closer—these were the planets. They spent centuries figuring out how these planets moved, and they cracked the complicated patterns in their movements. After a few thousand years, scientists finally figured out that these planets did not revolve around the Earth. They revolved around the Sun, completing an orbit every time they

How the Planets Formed

The universe is "lumpy"—mostly open space, with a lot of lumps of matter (stars, planets, and so forth). How did the lumps form in the first place? One good place to start looking for pieces of the puzzle is the solar system.

This particular story begins with a vast cloud of gas and dust that formed at least 5 billion years ago—and probably even earlier. There were **forces** acting on the cloud—gravity was pulling it inward, magnetic fields threaded through the gas and dust, and gas molecules pushed outward to help keep the cloud "inflated." Then, about 5 billion years ago, something, perhaps the explosion of a nearby star, caused the cloud to collapse.

As it collapsed, the cloud started to spin faster, and as it spun faster, it flattened into a spinning disk. The center of the disk became hot, forming what would become our Sun. Around the disk, the gas and dust began to clump together into larger and larger particles. Much of the material nearest the center of the disk was made of rock and metal, but it lost much of its gas because of the heat at the center. So, only rocky material could survive, forming the **terrestrial planets** Mercury, Venus, Earth, and Mars. The outer part of the disk had rock and metal, too, but they also kept their gas and ice; these eventually formed the **gas giants** such as Jupiter and Neptune. The center of the disk compressed, and from the compression it became so hot that it "ignited" into hydrogen fusion and became the Sun.

made a complete trip around the yellow star. By using the tools of mathematics, they could predict the orbits of the planets and where they would be at any future time in their journey around the Sun. Only by learning the rules of planetary motion could scientists launch spacecraft that could reach any planet.

Cassini was not the first probe to the outer solar system—the *Pioneer* and *Voyager* spacecraft had led the way as far as Neptune in the 1970s and 1980s. *Cassini* was not even the first probe to go into orbit around a giant planet in the outer reaches of the solar system—the *Galileo* spacecraft had accomplished that a few years earlier with Jupiter. But *Cassini* was the largest probe to be sent so far from home, the first to visit Saturn (*Pioneer* and *Voyager* merely passed through Saturn's system of moons), and it carried on board the *Huygens* probe, which would be the first human-made object to land on a major moon—Titan—in the outer solar system. This mission had been in the planning stages for decades; some scientists devoted their entire careers to planning and carrying out the mission. No wonder tension was running high at mission control.

It is easy to imagine a spacecraft's path as being a gently curved line that starts at Earth and ends up at the destination planet—like a golfer's putt to the cup. *Cassini*'s path was more like interplanetary pinball; two quick bank shots around Venus and a pivot around the Earth to set up an escape from the inner solar system. Then, a quick bumper shot off Jupiter, a long cruise to Saturn, and a final trapping maneuver at the destination. What made this possible, and what made the finale so incredibly, mind-bogglingly accurate, was scientists' detailed knowledge of planetary motions. It is easy to think of out-of-this-world comparisons for the feat that *Cassini* accomplished, but here is an example closer to home. Driving across town to visit a friend, a person might arrive five minutes earlier or later than planned, depending on traffic and traffic lights. *Cassini* spent nearly seven years traveling across the solar system and was closer to an on-time arrival than most trips to a nearby shopping mall.

Cassini is not the only spacecraft to play pinball with the solar system—in fact, every spacecraft that has traveled farther than Mars has done so, and even some missions to Venus and Mercury have taken a more roundabout route than one might guess. An understanding of planetary motion is certainly necessary to bounce around

Planetary Pinball

Every space probe that has traveled to the outer solar system has taken a roundabout path to get to its final destination. *Cassini* went past Venus, the Earth, and Jupiter to get to Saturn. *Galileo, Pioneer, Voyager,* and the *New Horizons* mission to Pluto, as well as the *Ulysses* mission to study the Sun and several probes to **comets** and **asteroids** have all used these gravity-assist maneuvers to help build up speed and to change direction. Here is why scientists do this and how it works.

There are two main reasons to play planetary pinball: to try to visit more places, and to try to reach a planet faster. In reality, scientists use the planets for both of these at the same time, taking advantage of the gravity of each planet and its motion through space.

The *Voyager 2* probe visited Jupiter, Saturn, Uranus, and Neptune. When *Voyager 2* was en route to the planets, they were not all lined up in a row—they were scattered through the solar system, with each planet moving through space at a different speed—and each one pulled on the *Voyager* as it went past. This pull is what changed the direction of the spacecraft as well as added speed.

Say a family is holding a sweet-16 party for their high school sophomore. As she walks in the door, she might want to head to the dining room because that is where all of her friends will be for the party. But as soon as she comes in, her mom stops her and tells her to put her coat in the closet—so she changes direction to put her coat in the closet. From there, she starts to walk toward the dining room again, but now her grandmother stops her in the family room to tell her how tall she has grown. The grandmother might hold her arm while she tells her a story, and then maybe she sends her over to talk to her grandfather on the other side of the room. By the time the girl finally

(continues)

(continued)

reaches the dining room, she may have been stopped by many of her family members, and each of them might have sent her in a different direction. So, her path to the dining room will be the result of all of her interactions with all of her relatives from the time she enters the room, each of whom has influenced her path from the front door to the dining room.

Scientists can do the same thing with a spaceship, except that they can plan the path in advance. Scientists know how hard Jupiter, for example, will pull on a spaceship, and they know how it will change the spaceship's path through space. So, they can arrange for a spaceship to pass by Jupiter at a precise place and time and along a precise path. They can calculate exactly how much of a pull Jupiter

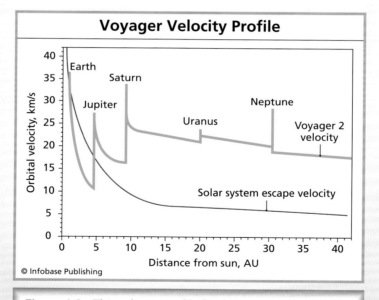

© Infobase Publishing

Figure 1.2   This velocity profile for the *Voyager 2* spacecraft shows how planets can affect a spacecraft's speed and direction.

will exert at every point of the trajectory, so they can also calculate the exact direction of the probe as it leaves Jupiter. Using all of this information, they can aim the ship so that, when it emerges from Jupiter's gravitational pull, it will be aimed toward its next destination. Once there, it will be redirected toward the next stop on its itinerary. This is how scientists use planets and their gravity to navigate around the solar system.

It is also possible to use planets to actually pick up speed, and scientists do this as well. In fact, *Galileo* and *Cassini* were big spacecraft—no rockets are strong enough to give them enough speed to reach the outer solar system in a relatively short time. But scientists can use the planets to speed them up as well as change their direction.

When a probe is in space approaching a planet, it is being pulled by the planet's gravity—it is falling toward the planet. As it falls, it speeds up, just as an apple falling to Earth will pick up speed. The probe's path will take it past the planet, so at some point, it will start to move away from the planet again; as it does so, it starts to slow down again. If all scientists do is "drop" a space probe past a planet, it will simply end up at the same speed it started with. This is due to a law of nature called the "conservation of energy," meaning that, if nothing else pushes or pulls the probe, it will neither gain nor lose energy through its journey.

The planet is also moving through space. If a probe is aimed "behind" a planet as the planet is moving through space, the probe is picking up speed due to the planet's gravity—this includes picking up the speed of the planet as it moves along its orbit. As the probe leaves the planet, it loses the speed it picked up from the planet's gravity but retains the extra speed the planet had as it moved along its orbit. Thus, the probe speeds up, letting it reach far-flung planets in a matter of years, rather than decades. In this sense, the gravity-assist maneuver is sort of like bouncing a ball off a moving target—a train, for example. Say a

(continues)

(continued)

commuter is standing on a platform and a train is coming at 50 miles per hour (80 km per hour, or kph). The commuter throws a ball at 30 miles per hour (48 kph) so that it hits the front of the train head-on, and it bounces off at a much higher speed. Here's what the ball and the train "see." From the train's perspective, the ball has hit it at a speed of 80 miles per hour (129 kph)—the 30 miles per hour of the ball plus the 50 miles per hour of the train. So, the ball bounces off the train, still traveling 80 miles per hour with respect to the train. But, since the train is still traveling at 50 miles per hour relative to the commuter on the train platform, the ball (which is moving at 80 miles per hour relative to the train) is now moving at 130 miles per hour (209 kph) with respect to the person on the platform. From the train's

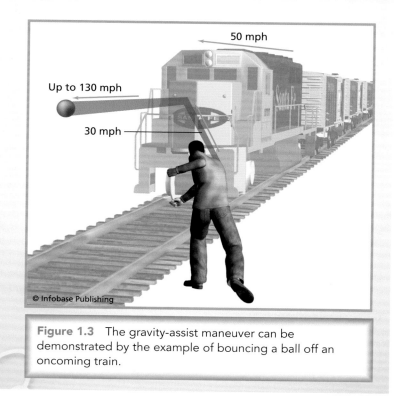

© Infobase Publishing

Figure 1.3 The gravity-assist maneuver can be demonstrated by the example of bouncing a ball off an oncoming train.

perspective, the ball has simply hit and bounced away. But, because the train is moving with respect to the person on the platform, the ball increases its speed from 30 to 130 miles per hour from the commuter's perspective. This is similar to what happens to a spaceship that picks up speed from both a planet's gravity (which it must lose again) and from the planet's motion through space (which it keeps).

the solar system, but even traveling to the Moon requires many more mathematical calculations than one might guess. In fact, one of the major reasons that the United States reached the Moon ahead of the Soviet Union was due to superior computer technology—the United States had the computer power to calculate everything needed to navigate to the Moon. Reaching the outer frontiers of the solar system would push science and technology even further.

FIRST ATTEMPTS

Although scientists have understood the basic laws of planetary motion for hundreds of years, it is only very recently that humans could take advantage of them to build spacecraft that could tour the solar system. More precisely, 1959 was the year that a spacecraft made it out of Earth's orbit, when the Soviet Union sent the *Luna 3* probe around the Moon to take photos of the far side. In addition to being a propaganda victory in the midst of the Cold War, it also returned valuable scientific information—for the first time in history, humankind knew what the other side of the Moon looked like and that it looked very different from the side seen from the Earth each night. Other lunar missions followed, by both American and Soviet craft, and by the middle of the 1960s, traveling to the Moon was fairly routine, at least by unmanned ships.

Scientists have sent craft to the outer reaches of the solar system; it seems silly to think that reaching the Moon might be difficult. But everything is difficult the first time around—and reaching the Moon was no different. The Moon travels along its orbit at a speed of 2,288 miles per hour (3,682 kph). During a three-day trip to the Moon, the Moon will travel over 80,000 miles (128,748 km) along its orbit. So, if a spacecraft simply aims for the Moon, by the time it reaches the Moon's orbit, the spacecraft will be far behind its target. This means that mission control specialists have to "lead" the Moon by aiming at where it will be when the craft reaches the lunar orbit, not at where it is at the time of the launch. So, that is part of the problem—the easiest part.

When a rock is thrown into the air, it rises, slows, stops, and falls back to Earth because the Earth's gravity is pulling it back; no person has the strength to throw a rock fast enough to escape the gravitational pull of the Earth. Spacecraft leaving the Earth still feel the effects of gravity just like the rock, although they are traveling quickly enough that they do not fall back to Earth. Instead of speeding up as they go into space, they slow down continuously as they leave the Earth, and the degree of slowing itself changes as the craft moves ever farther from the planet. At some point, the Moon's gravity will start pulling on the craft more strongly than does the Earth's and, at that point, the craft begins to pick up speed as it falls toward the Moon. All of these changes in speed must also be taken into account if the spacecraft is to reach its target at just the right time. If it misses this "window," the mission will fail. Too soon, and the Moon will not yet have arrived at the rendezvous point. Too late, and the meeting will have already passed. Like Goldilocks, everything has to be just right, or the mission will be a failure. In reality, it is even more complicated, because every body in the solar system is also pulling on the spacecraft. Now, for a simple mission to the Moon, scientists may only have to worry about the Sun, Moon, and Earth—but even three objects adds enough complication to make the problem very difficult to solve. It is bad enough to worry about a chunk of hardware, but when there are people riding inside the hardware, everything must be perfect. The U.S. advantage in computers during the 1960s made conditions safe enough for American astronauts to travel to the Moon.

As if hitting the Moon was not hard enough, in 1961 the Soviet Union aimed for Venus. With a longer travel time, trying to hit a faster-moving planet, and aiming closer to the Sun, it is not surprising that it took a few tries to succeed—in fact, the first successful Venus mission flew past the planet in 1963. After Venus came Mars, then Jupiter, Mercury, and the outer solar system. Each time, scientists were solving ever-more complicated computational problems, involving more planets and more difficult calculations. In the 1970s and 1980s, these experiences culminated in the "grand tour" of the *Voyager 2* probe, flying past Jupiter, Saturn, Uranus, and Neptune. In the 1990s and 2000s, NASA's *Galileo* and *Cassini* spacecraft began the in-depth explorations of Jupiter, Saturn, and their systems of moons. Every single one of these missions broke new ground in interplanetary navigation, and every one depended utterly on the ability to forecast, years in advance, the exact location of the spacecraft and the target planet, and the paths of the spacecraft amidst the pulls of every planet in the solar system.

FLYBYS AND ORBITS

A visit to a planet usually begins with a flyby (a mission in which the spacecraft flies past the planet being studied). After months or years in space, scientists may have only a few weeks to obtain data, and perhaps only a few hours at closest approach for the most important observations. This may seem like a colossal waste of time and money—why should nations spend billions of dollars and years of effort simply to get a few hours of time up close with the target? On the other hand, just reaching another planet is hard work, and those few precious hours provide an important opportunity to study it that is unavailable from Earth. In fact, not only can scientists gather a lot of good information in that short period of time, but they can actually bring more instruments to study a planet on a flyby mission—if the spacecraft is going to stick around, then it would need extra fuel to enter orbit. Since the whole spacecraft—fuel included—can only weigh so much, every pound of fuel means one fewer pound of instrumentation that can ride along. Spacecraft are packed like a family car going on vacation—every bit of room is filled with something; if the dog comes along, another family member may have to stay behind. Adding a 2-liter soda to the cooler may mean the milk has to stay home. On a spaceship, extra fuel means fewer instruments and less science that can be done.

That being said, there is an advantage in sticking around for a while—a flyby provides a short snapshot of what a planet looks like, but much more can be learned by watching things for months or years. So, as with *Cassini*, *Galileo*, and some Mars and Venus missions, scientists sometimes decide to put spacecraft into orbit. In the case of Jupiter and Saturn, this becomes a very sophisticated operation, because Jupiter and Saturn are both hosts to their own systems of moons (making them almost miniature versions of the solar system). Jupiter alone has four major moons, called

The Four Fundamental Forces in Nature

There are four fundamental forces in the universe. Two of them, the strong and the weak nuclear forces, matter most to things smaller than the size of atoms. The strong nuclear force helps to hold the cores of atoms together, and the weak nuclear force is involved in many radioactive decays.

Another force, **electromagnetism**, has a longer reach but weakens quickly, because it relies on the presence of electrical charge and magnetic fields. The universe as a whole is electrically and magnetically neutral (that is, the electrical and magnetic forces tend to cancel each other out), so electromagnetism cannot exert a truly long-range force.

The strength of the last force, gravity, changes with distance in the same way as electromagnetism. That is, it drops in strength by the square of the distance. So, for example, an object that doubles its distance from the Earth will feel the Earth's gravity drop by a factor of 2 squared, or 4. Of all the forces, gravity acts over the greatest distance, since there is nothing like positive and negative charges to cancel its effects. The entire universe dances to gravity's tune, and understanding how gravity works explains why *Cassini*'s path and arrival were so exquisitely precise.

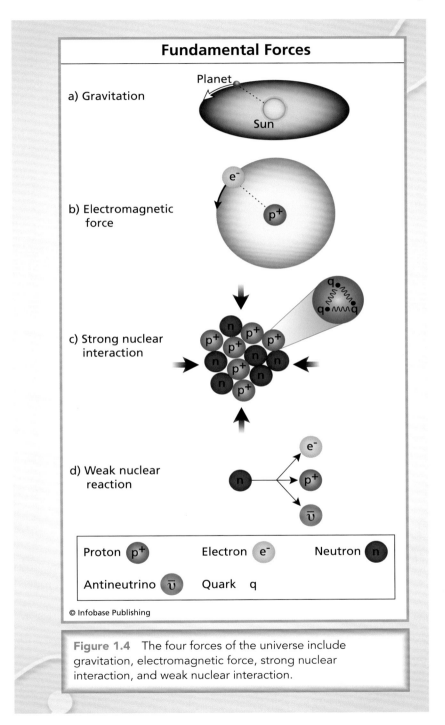

Fundamental Forces

a) Gravitation

Planet

Sun

b) Electromagnetic force

e⁻

p⁺

c) Strong nuclear interaction

q

q

q

n

p⁺

p⁺

p⁺

p⁺

n

n

n

p⁺

n

n

p⁺

d) Weak nuclear reaction

n

e⁻

p⁺

$\bar{\upsilon}$

Proton p⁺   Electron e⁻   Neutron n

Antineutrino $\bar{\upsilon}$ Quark q

© Infobase Publishing

Figure 1.4 The four forces of the universe include gravitation, electromagnetic force, strong nuclear interaction, and weak nuclear interaction.

the Galilean moons, each about the size of Earth's Moon. But that is not all—Jupiter has an ever-increasing number of small moons, or minor satellites. Moons are also called "satellites" because they orbit their mother planet, just as communications satellites orbit the Earth. Saturn reigns over an equally complicated system, and spacecraft have spent years exploring both of these systems. Doing this—moving into Jovian orbit and cruising among the Galilean moons and the rings of Jupiter, sending the *Huygens* probe to land on Saturn's moon Titan and crossing through Saturn's ring system—pushes the process of navigating a space probe through the gravitational fields of planets and moons to a whole new level. *Galileo, Cassini, Voyager, Magellan*, and other spacecraft have returned thousands of beautiful photos, and their discoveries will keep scientists busy for decades. These craft have also shown that scientists know how to use the laws of planetary motion to navigate around the solar system, and this is no less important than Christopher Columbus and Ferdinand Magellan learning to use the stars, the Sun, the winds, the currents, and the tides to learn how to navigate around the Earth.

This book will explain how the planets move and will reveal the laws that govern their motions through the sky. The story of our understanding of the planets' motion began thousands of years ago, when ancient astronomers attempted to puzzle out the motions of a few wandering "stars" that were different from the rest of the dots in the night sky. These scientists made mistakes, but their mistakes often paved the way for new discoveries. Famous scientists Johannes Kepler, Edmond Halley, Isaac Newton, and others discovered the laws of gravity and planetary motion and learned to use these laws to explain the workings of the solar system. The laws they discovered enable space probes to find their way from planet to planet and may make it possible for human beings eventually to visit planets in person. Yet, scientists and mathematicians in more recent times have learned that even science and math have limits—thanks to a phenomenon called chaos, the position of most planets cannot be predicted more than a few million years into the future. Remarkably, the same laws for planets operate on a galactic and a universal scale—the exact same laws that govern the Moon's path around the Earth also predict the path of Earth's home galaxy—the Milky Way—as it travels among its more than 35 neighboring galaxies—which scientists call the **Local Group of galaxies**.

With thousands of years and billions of light-years to travel, it ought to be an exciting trip. Time to get started!

2

The First Astronomers

On a clear night, it is easy to see that the stars are arranged in what seem to be lots of patterns—dots of light against the black of the sky. Through the ages, people have seen shapes in these patterns—bears, dogs, plows, lions, snakes, and more. These are the constellations. The names of the constellations may have changed over time, but their shapes have remained the same through all of human history. The stars remain in the same positions and they form the same shapes today that they did for the ancient Greeks and Egyptians thousands of years ago, except for a few, and those are the ones that are most important in this book.

People have always looked to the sky, and they have likely always wondered about what they saw. At some point in the distant past, someone—an unknown person who became the first astronomer—began to notice that the stars moved through the sky. This first astronomer, and many who followed, began to follow these motions. From dawn to dusk, the Sun (and sometimes the Moon) moved from horizon to horizon. It moved in a giant circular path, or arc. From dusk to dawn, a multitude of stars moved across the sky, each following its own arc. These first astronomers would have noticed that the stars changed from season to season as well—the stars they could see in the summer were different from those they could see in the winter. Finally, they would have noticed that almost every object in the sky followed the same sort of path, moving from east to west, and almost every object in the sky followed a separate path—only rarely did any of the lights come together in the sky. And they would have noticed one thing that did not change—that almost every one of the stars kept the same position with respect to all of the other stars.

People must have wondered about the stars from the earliest days—wondered what they were and why they moved through the skies in the way that they do. Today, astronomers can explain all of these motions. The Earth rotates around an imaginary line through its center—its **axis**. When the Earth rotates one complete turn around its axis, that equals a day. As the Earth rotates, people on the ground see the stars rise in the east and set in the west. Another type of motion takes place—the motion of the Earth around the Sun. This motion—one full trip around the Sun, which equals a year—causes the constellations to change with the seasons. The earliest astronomers would not have known these things, so they could not explain the motion of the stars in this manner; but they did come up with some explanations that made sense to them—explanations that described the motion of almost all of the stars.

What they had more trouble figuring out were the motions of the strange stars—the ones whose movements seemed to be connected to other strange stars. These strange stars moved in and out of the constellations, seemingly according to some plan of their own. Nobody understood where these wandering stars came from, why they moved, or what drove their motions through the sky. What they did know was that there were five of these things—today called Mercury, Venus, Mars, Jupiter, and Saturn—and they wanted to know more about them.

Today, people know these things are planets, but the quest to reach this understanding took thousands of years, and its consequences were profound. When humans first undertook this quest, they thought they were at the geographical center of the universe. Now, thousands of years later, people realize they are living on a small planet circling a little star in a galactic suburb.

ANCIENT CIVILIZATIONS

To the ancient Egyptians (about 1600 B.C. or so), the planets were gods that sailed through the heavens in small boats. Unlike the

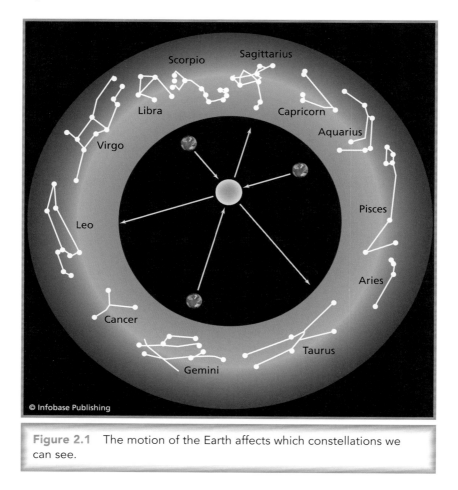

Figure 2.1   The motion of the Earth affects which constellations we can see.

"fixed" stars (the stars that did not move with respect to each other), the planets were always moving—for this reason, they were called "the stars that know no rest." But, to the Egyptians, the divine planets moved according to their own laws, not people's laws. Their motions might be predicted, but it was not man's place to tell the gods how to move.

The Babylonians (circa 600 B.C.), an ancient civilization that lived in what is now Iraq, saw things a little differently. The planets were still gods to them, but their movements revealed their plans. By understanding and being able to interpret the motions of the planets, the Babylonians hoped they would be able to understand what the gods wanted and what they were going to do next. So, predicting where the gods were going to be—where they would appear in the sky, when and where they would rise and set—became critically important. It was the only way the Babylonians thought that they could try to understand their gods. In this quest for understanding, the Babylonian priests developed a system of mathematics and one of the most sophisticated calendars of the ancient world. Ultimately, the Babylonians were not interested in explaining what they saw; they only wanted to be able to know where to look for their gods.

When the ancient Chinese looked to the skies thousands of years ago, they did not see gods, unlike astronomers in other parts of the world. What they saw made them think, instead, of their emperor and their government. Instead of creating a mythology around the stars and planets, Chinese astronomers were satisfied simply to see and to describe what was there. They noticed the same patterns and the same rhythms; they just did not associate these with their gods. They did, however, believe that events in the heavens could affect life on Earth—but they attributed this to mythological animals and forces instead of gods. As a result, Chinese astronomers calculated the length of the day and the year, and the amount of time between **eclipses**—bizarre events in which the Sun or Moon became completely covered in shadows—to very high degrees of accuracy. They mentioned celestial events that escaped the notice of European astronomers even into the Middle Ages.

The Greeks and Their Epicycles

The ancient Greeks also looked to the skies. Influenced by the Babylonians, the Greeks also saw gods in the skies. Unlike the Babylonians, however, the Greeks wanted desperately to know what was going on—they wanted to know how and why the planets moved as they did. What the Greeks came up with ended up lasting more than 1,000 years.

To the Greeks, as explained best by the philosopher Aristotle, the universe was a series of crystal spheres, and the planets and stars were attached to these spheres. Each sphere moved a little differently, and their motions could explain how stars and planets moved.

With time, this view of the planets changed further, and by the second century B.C., the Greeks had developed a more complex view of the universe. They realized that a simple set of spheres could not explain why, sometimes, some of the planets would seem to move backward, or why only some of the planets had this **retrograde motion**. By about 200 B.C, the philosopher Apollonius of Perga realized

The Pyramids and Plate Tectonics

When the pyramids were first studied, archaeologists and other scientists were amazed to find that they are lined up almost perfectly in the north-south direction. In fact, the Great Pyramid of Khufu is only a tiny fraction of 1 degree away from perfect alignment. The Egyptians did this without having any modern technology—no satellites, no maps of the world—to tell them where the Earth's north and south poles were located. To put this in further perspective, this is twice as accurate as buildings constructed nearly 4,000 years later. Maybe they lined up the pyramids in relation to some stars that indicated the location of the north and south poles. Even with this high degree of precision, there were some who wondered why the alignment was not perfect—why did the Egyptians not do even better?

First, consider how precise the alignment is—the Great Pyramid is about 3.4 arc minutes away from true north. There are 360 degrees in a full circle, and 60 arc minutes in one degree. Therefore, 3.4 arc minutes is about $1/18$ of 1 degree. So, how well did the ancient Egyptians do in pointing to the stars?

Well, the size of the Moon in the sky is about ½ degree. Imagine that a rocket follows the exact path that the Great Pyramid is now pointing. Instead of arriving directly at the center of the Moon, the rocket would land a little to the right of the center—about $1/10$ of the distance between the exact center and the very edge of the Moon. Or, another that all of this could be explained with what he called **epicycles**. His system was refined in the next century by another early Greek scientist, Hipparchus of Nicaea, and perfected in the first century A.D. by the great astronomer Ptolemy (pronounced "toe-le-may"), but the general concept lasted for centuries. Of course, this brings up the question, "what's an epicycle?"—a very good question indeed.

way to look at it is that if an airplane flew from New York City to Seattle (about 2,400 miles, or 3,862 km), and if the airplane was aimed 3.4 arc minutes away from the center of the runway at the airport, the plane would land about 2.5 miles (4 km) away from where it aimed—the craft would probably still touch down (although with some bumps) on the grounds of the airport. In fact, in some larger airports, it could simply land on another runway.

Maybe the pyramids were once aligned with the north and south more perfectly, but perhaps natural events slightly shifted their position over the past few thousand years. Some possibilities include tidal waves (tsunamis), volcanoes, earthquakes, and more. The most interesting explanation was that maybe plate tectonics—the motion of the continents across the face of the Earth—might be responsible. Egypt, like every other part of the world, is on a great tectonic plate that moves across the Earth. Although in any single year the plates only move an inch (2.5 centimeters, or cm) or so, over thousands of years it was thought that these slight movements might have moved the Great Pyramid out of alignment. Alas, this turns out not to be the case. The African plate is, indeed, in motion, and it has actually moved more than 65 feet (20 m) in the 4,500 years since the Great Pyramid was built. But the angle of the plate has changed by only a small fraction of what would be needed to explain the orientation of the Great Pyramid—the ancient Egyptians simply were not perfect. But they were still very good.

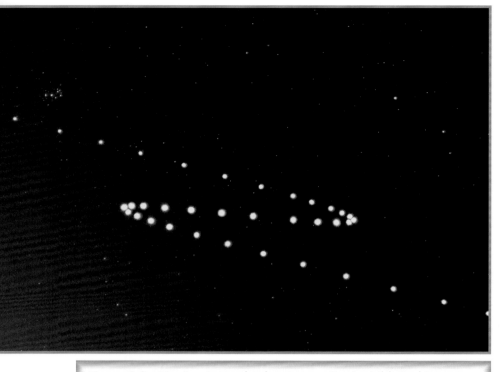

Figure 2.2 Mars's retrograde planetary motion is visible in this composite photo taken over the course of several weeks.

What occurred to Apollonius was that the motion of the planets through the sky could be explained if they followed two sets of motions that were superimposed, or lay on top of, each other. He thought that the planets might be moving in a small circle, and that the center of this small circle was moving in a larger circle through the sky. The large circle is called the deferent, and the small circle is called the epicycle. The planet moves around the epicycle, and the epicycle, in turn, moves around the deferent. When the planet is moving along the top part of the epicycle, it is moving "forward" through the sky. Its retrograde motion happens when it reaches the bottom part of the epicycle, moving "backward" against the fixed stars in the sky. Epicycles are complicated, but they were the only way that the earliest astronomers could think of to make everything work—at least, the only way if the Earth was the center of the universe.

What Is a Planet?

To the Greeks, this was an easy question to answer—the Greek word *planet* means something that drifts or wanders. So, to the Ancient Greeks, a planet was something that wandered across the stars in the sky. This definition held up fairly well until the early 1800s, when astronomers began discovering asteroids. The first asteroid to be identified, Ceres (which was recently reclassified as a "dwarf" planet), was discovered in 1801, and it was promptly called a planet. Then, more asteroids were found; first a few, then hundreds, and now we know of tens of thousands of asteroids. After the count had risen a bit, astronomers realized that these could not *all* be planets. About the same time, they began to realize that these new objects were also fairly small—they were renamed "asteroids."

In the late 1800s and early 1900s, astronomers noticed discrepancies in the orbital motions of Neptune and Uranus, and they began looking for more distant planets. Planet number nine, Pluto, was discovered in 1930 by Clyde Tombaugh, and schoolchildren everywhere learned the names of the nine planets.

Fast-forwarding to the 1990s, astronomers began finding a lot of objects beyond Neptune, some of which rivaled Pluto in size. As with the asteroids, astronomers and planetary scientists began questioning whether or not Pluto really deserved to be called a planet, given its diminutive size and its crowded neighborhood. In 2006, the International Astronomical Union (IAU) finally came up with a formal definition of a planet—an object that is in orbit around the Sun, that is large enough to form itself into a spherical shape, and that has "cleared the neighborhood" of all other objects in its orbit. Pluto meets the first two of these criteria (as do several of the largest asteroids), but fails the third test. So, as of 2006, Pluto is considered a "dwarf planet," and our solar system now has eight full planets.

ANCIENT OBSERVATORIES

People usually think of an observatory as being a building with a giant telescope pointed at the sky. Observatories today are temples of a sort—temples of science to which astronomers from the

Figure 2.3 Though people tend to think science and religion are opposites, the ancient Temple of the Sun in Machu Picchu (*above*), was used for observation, just as are modern observatories like the Keck telescope (*opposite page*) in Hawaii.

entire world come to learn about the heavens. The astronomers are there to learn about the stars, galaxies, and the universe. They seek to answer the most fundamental questions about how the universe works, how it began, and how what happens in the skies might affect the Earth. In this pursuit, astronomers use the best tools and the most advanced technology available to science. To that extent, observatories today are not unlike those built by ancient civilizations. It is not easy to see similarities between ancient temples such as Stonehenge, Machu Picchu, Angkor Wat, and today's modern telescope farm at the top of Mauna Kea, but they are there. Take away the tools—the computers, the stones, the telescopes—and look at the people, and there are more similarities than differences, because the ancient astronomers were also on a quest to try to learn how the universe began, how it works, and how it affects people here on Earth. Every civilization tries to answer these same questions, using the tools they are capable of making. Telescopes or stones—the tools differ, but the motivation and the quest are the same.

It is true that many of the ancient observatories were also religious centers, while today, people tend to think that science and religion are opposites. But the ancient world had no scientists—it was the priests whose job was to try to understand the heavens. Knowing

this makes it easy to see that the purpose of Stonehenge was similar to the purpose of the Keck telescope in Hawaii—to try to observe the heavens, to try to learn more, and to try to put that understanding to use here on Earth.

There is one fundamental difference between modern observatories and those of the ancient world, however—unlike modern observatories, the ancient observatories tended to rely on walls, windows, and other features that line up with astronomically important points. Examples of this abound in the temples of the ancient Maya civilization, one of the most advanced civilizations that lived in Central and South America thousands of years ago. In the Maya temple/observatory of Chichén Itzá, in the structure known as El Caracol, Venus appears on the horizon in a particular window exactly every eight years. In another structure on this site, now named El Castillo, the Sun shining through a window creates a snake-shaped shadow on the equinox, when the Sun is directly over the equator, but no other time. Some of these astronomical events may have had a practical significance, possibly associated with good times to plant or harvest crops (and farmers still talk of the "harvest moon" today); others had religious significance.

The Maya Calendar

Any calendar marks cycles, and all calendars are based on astronomy. One month marks the approximate amount of time it takes the Moon to circle the Earth. A year is the amount of time it takes the Earth to go around the Sun. At the end of the year, the cycle begins again. The calendar is a numerical cycle—going from 1 to 365 and then starting again—and it marks the physical cycle of the Earth circling the Sun from one point and back to that point in space again. Every planet will have its own unique "natural" calendars, based on its own year and its own satellites. The Maya realized this; they probably realized it better than people do today. Their astronomical observations of the planets (especially Venus) gave them a deep understanding of the cycles of the Earth, Moon, Sun, and Venus. From this, the Maya created a calendar that is unequaled for its complexity and its scope.

The Maya had many calendars, each serving a different purpose, and these calendars could be combined in any number of ways. They began with a 260-day calendar that was the most important. They also used a 365-day calendar—just like the yearly calendar. Both of these could be combined into a "Calendar Round" that lasted for 52 years—the amount of time until both cycles returned to zero at the same time. To these calendars, the Maya added 13-day and 20-day cycles, and more. Finally, there was the Long Count calendar, which was not a cycle, but was more like a time line (or a number line). The Long Count calendar could be used to keep track of historical events—to keep track of what happened in the past. All of these calendars were based on observations of the Sun, Moon, and planets.

All of these calendars sound confusing, but the modern calendar system would probably confuse the Maya. After all, modern society now has a 7-day cycle (Monday, Tuesday, Wednesday, Thursday, Friday, Saturday, Sunday) that makes up one week. A month is a 28-, 30-, or 31-day cycle, and a year consists of a 365- (or 366-) day cycle. Not only that, but the calendar year runs from January 1 until December 31, while school calendars run from late August or early September until sometime in May or June. All of these are based on cycles, just like the Maya cycle calendars. In addition, people also use a modern version of the Maya Long Count calendar—dates and years. The days, weeks, and months cycle by, endlessly repeating— just like a wheel spinning around and around. It is only by keeping track of the years, the times that the wheel completes a spin, that people can tell the difference between March 14 of this year compared to March 14, 1997.

ASTROLOGY AND ASTRONOMY

On the door of an office in a university astronomy department there is a notice: "If you call an astronomer an astrologer, you're the one who will be seeing stars!" Today, people make a clear distinction between astronomy and astrology. Astronomy is in a museum or on a science show. Astrology is in the horoscopes section, next to the comics, or something practiced by a fortune-teller who promises to predict the future.

Astronomy is a science, a systematic way of describing nature, one that makes predictions that can be tested. Astrology is most kindly called a "pseudo-science"; a collection of beliefs that have no basis in science, but that pretend to be scientific because they are based on celestial motions. The quote is correct—mix up astrology and astronomy in the presence of a scientist (especially an astronomer), and the scientist will probably not be too happy. Today, astrology gets very little respect from scientists, and astrologers seem to spend most of their time advising people on romance and job-seeking. In fact, when it was revealed in 1988 that an astrologer was giving advice to President Ronald Reagan's wife, Nancy, many people laughed at her and believed she was being ignorant and gullible.

It has not always been like that, though. In fact, it is only within the past few centuries that there has been a clear distinction between the two, and at times in the past, astrologers were given a tremendous amount of power, advising kings and emperors, designing buildings, and even predicting the best time to make war. To understand why, it is important to remember that people in the ancient world saw things very differently than we do today.

Imagine, for example, a Maya king. He is doing his best to rule his people wisely. At first, his kingdom is flourishing and healthy. Then, there is a drought. For reasons beyond his control, crops die, game animals move elsewhere, and his people begin to starve. In a short time, his kingdom is in ruins, and he asks himself why. He was a compassionate king, his people loved him, and his allies trusted him. He was also a powerful king, and his enemies knew enough to leave him alone. He tried to lead a good life and to take care of his people. In spite of all of this, his kingdom still failed. At times like this, it is only natural for him to think that he is being punished for something that is wrong with him—that the gods looked inside his heart and saw something that they did not like. So, he thinks they caused the rains to stop.

If he is like most in the ancient world, he would look to the skies to see the gods, or to see evidence of their work. As a king, he would call for his court astrologer, his high priest, or for whoever studies the skies in his kingdom and in his culture, and he would ask them to help him understand what was going on, and how to regain his former status. Eventually, after studying the positions of the planets and the stars and thinking deeply about what it all means, they might have an answer for him. As time goes by, the rains return and, with them, his kingdom's prosperity and power.

Going through all of this affects him. He is sorry that he displeased the gods, and he is happy that his astrologers were able, by predicting the positions of the planets, to tell him how to please them again. So, to make sure he does not make any other mistakes, perhaps he elevates the astrologer to a higher position. He may begin to ask for advice, to ask if the planets are in a good position to wage war or to plant crops. By and by, the astrologers become important advisors to him and, eventually, to his successor. If the gods are in the heavens, if the study of the heavens can help him to understand what they want, then a person who can help him to understand the heavens is going to be incredibly important. To his mind, astrologers and their advice are important tools, important weapons, and he would be foolish to ignore their advice. In ancient times, understanding the stars seemed to be crucial for staying in power and for surviving into the next year.

Compare this to today's world. Nowadays, astronomers try to understand the universe simply for the sake of knowing more about it. They are not studying astronomy to keep leaders in power or to figure out the best time to plant crops. Today's world is a special place compared to the ancient world. In today's world, astronomy does not often provide any immediate tangible benefit. Understanding how planets form will not help nations to win wars. It will not help to feed people, and no person will be elected president promising to help the public learn more about the universe. But as science keeps revealing interesting things about the universe, it provides unexpected benefits that humankind's ancestors never imagined. Developing telescopes for outer space—such as the Hubble Space Telescope—helped lead to cheap, widely available digital cameras for taking pictures here on Earth. While people now know the stars do not have minds of their own, understanding the motions of objects in space may someday help humanity to prevent dangerous asteroids from striking the Earth.

In the ancient world, the study of the planetary and stellar motions—astrology—was one of the many tools that rulers could use to help them stay in power, rule wisely, and expand their kingdoms. Astrologers, whether or not they realized it, were tracking the stars and planets so they could tell their leaders when new seasons began and when to expect changes of weather.

Although there is no way of knowing when people first realized that the planets move across the sky differently than the stars, historians do know that, by the time of the ancient Egyptians, Babylonians, and Greeks, the planets were recognized to be different and powerful. Whether they were viewed as gods or as portents of things to come, the planets were important, and it became important to be able to determine where they were and where they were going to be. Every culture developed its own **cosmology**—its own view of the how the universe worked—and every culture placed a great deal of importance on this cosmology and on those who could understand and interpret the motions of the planets across the sky.

A Better Set of Rules

*Philosophy is written in this grand book—I mean the
Universe—which stands continually open to our gaze,
but it cannot be understood unless one first learns to compre-
hend the language and interpret the characters in which it is
written. It is written in the language of mathematics, and its
characters are triangles, circles and other geometrical figures,
without which it is humanly impossible to understand
a single word of it.*
—Galileo Galilei

Imagine waking up one morning in a strange place—a large building with many rooms of different sizes. Suddenly, with little
warning, people begin streaming in, talking in a strange language,
some laughing, some looking worried, and all in a rush. In a few
minutes, everyone has sorted themselves out and each person is
sitting in a particular room, in a particular chair, doing something.
Sometime later, everyone suddenly gets out of their chairs to flood
back into the hallway and sort themselves into another room, where
they again sit down. This happens over and over again until, with no
apparent warning, everyone simply leaves. The next day, the whole
thing happens again, and again the next day and the next day. Then,
everyone is gone for two whole days.

As time goes on, it might be worthwhile to follow individual people—where does this person go? Who else goes to these same rooms? Are there any groups of people who all follow the same path? It might also be helpful to look for patterns in the movements—maybe everyone sits still for 55 minutes and there are 5-minute periods when they are in motion, perhaps they arrive and leave at the same time every day, and possibly they all eat in the same place at the same time. There is a limit to what can be learned, however, because they speak a strange language and it is impossible to ask them any questions. Eventually, after many hours of observation, there might seem to be an explanation for what is happening: These people are all artists, taking inspiration from the leader in their room! They come to work in the morning, and they spend the day painting small works of art. But being in the same place for a whole day can be boring, so every so often, everyone moves to a different room so they can have fresh surroundings and a new leader. Now everything makes sense—there may be a few small things still to explain, but those details do not seem important. Of course, this idea cannot be checked very well because it is impossible actually to talk to anyone. But the explanation seems to fit.

Then, one day, a dictionary appears, making it possible to understand the language—to listen, to talk, and to learn. Imagine the surprise when it becomes clear these people are not in an art factory after all—nobody is making art; they are all students in a school. This is a surprise, but it also explains everything—and it explains everything better than the earlier idea. It is still not possible to learn what is being taught, however, because the language, with all its rules, remains hard to decipher. Plus, it is not possible to tell the difference between their science, language, and history classes. Some small things may still be confusing—why does one person never show up at lunch, why do some people leave early, why do some arrive by bus and others walk, and so forth. At first, these questions cannot be asked because the language is still too hard to understand; as knowledge of the language improves, it is possible to learn more. Eventually, it seems that everything can be explained.

SPEAKING IN MATH   .

For nearly 2,000 years—from the time of Aristotle until the late 1500s—humans had a working understanding of how everything in the universe functioned. People thought that they had it all figured out, except for a few odds and ends. Aristotle had explained, for example, that a heavier ball fell faster than a lighter one. He had also explained that it was natural to move up and down—like jumping into a pool—but that moving horizontally—such as swimming across a pool—was unnatural. Everyone understood that the planets, the Sun, and the stars all circled around the Earth, with some of the planets following epicycles (which explained their occasional reversed motion through the sky). Aristotle taught that everything in the heavens was perfect and was unchanging. This view of the universe was accepted by many religions, by kings (when they bothered to think of such things), and by the intellectuals of the day.

In the late 1500s, this began to change—people began to question Aristotle. First, there was a "new" star—it is now called a supernova—that appeared in the skies in 1572. Aristotle's cosmology—his vision of how the universe works—had no room for anything new in the skies. The new star just did not fit. Just a few years later, another new object appeared: the great comet of 1577. Not only did the comet appear in the heavens, but it had a path that could be traced through the sky. Tycho Brahe, the last of the great pre-telescope astronomers, found that the comet broke many of Aristotle's laws: It was more distant than the Moon, its path was not a perfect circle, and its path took it through the various crystal spheres that Aristotle thought held the Sun, stars, and planets in place. In short, the comet and the supernova exploded the idea that the skies were eternally unchanging.

Simon Stevin, a mathematician and engineer, found out in 1586 that heavy things fell just as quickly as light things. The scientist Galileo Galilei made the same discovery a few years later. By itself, this was not really a big deal, but it showed that Aristotle had made a mistake, and it made it easier to wonder if he might have been wrong about other things, too. Stevin and Galileo were not the first to think so—both were preceded by Nicolaus Copernicus, who,

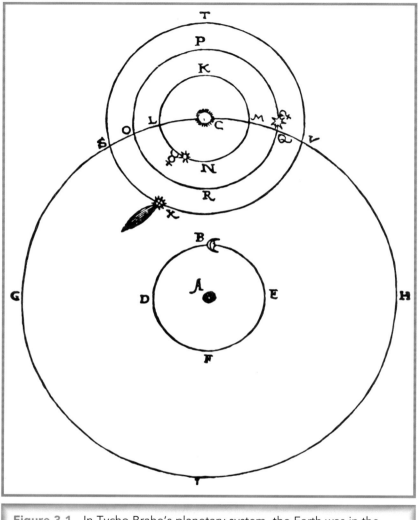

Figure 3.1 In Tycho Brahe's planetary system, the Earth was in the middle, the Sun rotated around the Earth, and the other planets rotated around the Sun. (Here, x shows the comet of 1577.)

in 1543, had published his theories of the motions of the universe. Copernicus described a universe in which the Earth was no longer the center, a universe in which the Earth was simply one of several planets that circled the Sun, and in which all planets followed simple orbits around the Sun.

Tycho Brahe

Without a doubt, one of the most interesting figures in sixteenth-century science was Tycho Brahe. As a scientist, he was among the last, and possibly the greatest, of the "naked eye" astronomers—the last generation of astronomers before the advent of telescopes. Tycho spent years making painstaking observations of the stars and planets with his own eyes, trying to accept the mathematical beauty of the **Copernican system**—the idea that the Sun was at the center of the solar system—while still keeping the Earth at the center of the universe. Although his ideas turned out to be wrong, his observations were so precise that they made possible Johannes Kepler's later discoveries on planetary motion. There is no doubt that Tycho was a great astronomer, and there is no doubt he was also one of a long line of scientists who have had colorful personal lives as well. In fact, he may well be one of the most colorful characters to work in science.

The colorful part of Tycho's history begins with his losing part of his nose in a duel as a college student. For the rest of his life, he wore a false nose that was made of metal. Inheriting a fortune from his adoptive uncle, Tycho owned an island, where he had a castle, his observatory, and a pet moose (and lived with a dwarf who Tycho thought had psychic abilities). The moose later died, falling down the stairs after drinking too much beer one day at dinner. Tycho died at the age of 55, although the exact cause is not known for sure. The story for at least a few centuries was that he died of a bladder infection, but recent studies show that he had dangerous levels of mercury in his body—it could be that he was poisoned, and there are some who think that it may have been Tycho's student, Johannes Kepler. Kepler certainly had the opportunity to do it, and he benefited from the use of Tycho's data archives after his death. For now, though, historians just do not know—and may never know—exactly what happened.

After this, changes came even more quickly. Copernicus had developed the mathematics to describe his system of the heavens, and he was followed by Johannes Kepler's calculations of planetary orbits in 1609. In 1610, Galileo began observing the skies through his new telescope and, after his observations, there was no turning back. From that time on, even though some people still fought the new ideas, Copernicus, Stevin, Kepler, Brahe, and Galileo had proved that Aristotle was wrong, that the Earth was not the center of the universe, and that the positions of every object in the sky could be predicted using mathematical calculations.

This last point is vitally important—mathematics could be used to predict the motions of the planets. This is why Galileo made the

Kepler's Universe

Whether Kepler actually killed Tycho or not, there is no doubt he was another great scientist whose work was a significant improvement in humankind's understanding of the motions of the planets. Unlike Tycho, Kepler firmly believed that Copernicus's theories were correct; Kepler wanted to figure out how it all worked by having the Sun sit at the middle of the solar system. This quest eventually led him to develop his laws of planetary motion.

Although many of Kepler's ideas and theories later turned out to be wrong, he had some good ideas that set the stage for the later work of future scientists such as Edmond Halley, Isaac Newton, and Robert Hooke. This work helped them to make their discoveries. Science is like a chain of discovery—Tycho's work led to Kepler's, whose discoveries led to Newton's, and so forth. This chain started with the first people to try to figure out how the world and the universe work, and it has continued through every scientist and every person since that time who has tried to understand more. Scientists learn from those who came before them, add to that knowledge if they can, and then teach this to the next generation of scientists, continuing this chain of learning and discovery.

comment quoted at the beginning of this chapter—the language of the universe is written in mathematics, and if humans are really to understand how the universe works, how the planets move, they must be able to understand the mathematics behind it.

As the story at the beginning of this chapter illustrates, it is difficult to understand something new at first. After many days of watching everyone hard at work, it was possible to come up with a theory about what they were doing. Since they spoke a strange language, however, it was difficult to check if the theory was correct. Obtaining a dictionary of their language and better decoding their conversations led to another, simpler, and more correct explanation for what they were doing. It was just necessary to understand their language. This is like the state of astronomy over the course of human history—people were perfectly happy with their understanding of how the universe worked, until they began to learn its language. Once people began to apply their new understanding of mathematics to the universe, it became obvious that the old cosmology was wrong. But until people invented the correct mathematics, they simply could not understand what they were seeing. Or, to look at it another way, the discovery and creation of new mathematical tools made it possible to come to a better understanding of what the telescopes showed astronomers about the stars.

For nearly a century, this is where things stood—all the planets (including the Earth) revolved around the Sun, they traveled in nearly circular orbits, and the planets' positions could be calculated in advance. The early scientists could see *what* was happening, but they were not yet sure about *why* or *how* it all worked. Scientists needed more language lessons—they needed better mathematics.

This set the stage for the next breakthrough by one of the greatest geniuses of all time—Isaac Newton.

ISAAC NEWTON'S UNIVERSE

Isaac Newton, by all accounts, was a miserable human being. He could be mean to his enemies, he could be nasty to talk with, and he would try to ruin men he thought to be his competitors. He was not the sort of person anyone would want to invite to a party. Newton spent only a part of his life working in what is now called "science."

The rest was spent dabbling in alchemy (a pursuit that included trying to convert ordinary metals into gold), writing about religion, helping to run the English treasury, and helping to restart and run the Royal Academy of Sciences. In between all of this, he helped to invent major chunks of mathematics, physics, and astronomy.

Actually, Newton worked at about the same time as another Englishman, Edmond Halley—the man for whom Halley's Comet is named. Halley noticed a regular pattern in the dates of some great comets that had been seen throughout history. He thought it was an interesting coincidence that every 76 years there was a great comet in the skies—and in about the same patch of the skies. To Halley, it made more sense to think that instead of a series of identical comets that showed up in the same place every 76 years, maybe there was a simply a single comet that had a 76-year orbit. Going out on a limb, Halley predicted in 1705 that there would be a great comet in 1758 (he turned out to be correct, but died before it returned).

Again—all of these astronomers could predict exactly where they expected to find the planets from year to year, and their predictions were correct. But nobody knew why. That is where Newton comes in.

In 1665, the Black Death struck England. Victims suffered horribly, and most of them died. The plague was much more concentrated in the cities than in the countryside, so Isaac Newton decided to leave Cambridge University for the country. Being an inquisitive sort of professor, Newton used his time to think about why the planets move the way that they do.

One of Newton's first realizations was that he did not have the right tools for the job—his mathematical "language" was not up to the task of describing the universe. So, before Newton could make any progress in his astronomy, he had to invent a new form of mathematics—what is called "calculus" today (calculus is the branch of mathematics that lets us describe how things move or how they change).

After inventing calculus, Newton again turned his attention to planetary motions. He knew that gravity was involved somehow, but this realization was not enough by itself. Newton's breakthrough came when he realized that every single object pulls on every other object. In other words, the Earth's gravity pulls an apple to the ground. But that is not all. The apple's gravity also tries to pull the

Earth toward it. Now, in the case of an apple and the Earth, the pull of the apple is not very large; certainly not large enough to cause the Earth to move in any noticeable way. But if two planets are roughly

The Three-body Problem: Chaos Enters the Solar System

Newton's law of gravity can determine the exact gravitational pull of any object on any other object with only a few bits of information: how far apart the two objects are from each other and how massive each of them is. Armed with this information, anyone can calculate the pull of the Sun's gravity, for example, on a planet in the solar system. Knowing how fast an object is moving can also help to predict its orbit—how it is moving through space around another object. When Newton first announced his laws of gravity and of motion, some scientists thought that it was only a matter of time until people could accurately predict the location and speed of every object in the universe, then and until the end of time. It turns out that it is not quite that easy—with more than two objects in the picture, it is not possible to calculate the precise position of each one of them forever into the future. This is called the "three-body problem," and here is why it is such a problem.

Say there are two objects—maybe the Earth and the Moon—sitting in space. Newton's law can calculate the pull of each on the other and their speeds, and it can even predict with confidence where each one of them will be until the end of time. It is easy, because there is only one object pulling on the Earth (the Moon), and vice versa. Even here, the motion is surprisingly complicated. It turns out that the Moon does not exactly orbit around a stationary Earth; instead, both Earth and Moon orbit around a common point—the **center of mass** of the Earth-Moon system. Because the Earth is more than 80 times as massive as the Moon, the Earth wobbles very slightly around the

(continues)

(continued)

center of its **mass**, while the Moon has a large orbit around the same center of mass. Imagine a father picking up his young daughter and spinning her around in a big circle. Even though the little girl is doing most of the moving, the father would be moving a little, too, maybe wobbling back and forth a little bit—this is the same thing that happens when the Moon orbits the Earth.

Now, say there is a third massive object near the Earth and Moon. The Earth pulls on this third object, which pulls back on the Earth. The Earth pulls on the Moon, too, which is also pulling on the Earth. The Moon and the third object are also both pulling on each other. So, there are three objects, each trying to pull on the other two. If the third object is close to the Earth, it might pull on the Earth more than the Moon does, and the Earth will return the favor. But, when the object moves closer to the Moon, it might pull the Moon farther away from the Earth, and the Moon's pull on Earth will drop for a while. Everything is pulling on everything, and the strength of that pull changes with distance. Over time, the movement of each of these objects grows more and more complex and increasingly hard to predict. So, even with only three nearby objects, it is never possible to predict perfectly where they will be forever—but it is possible to come close enough to launch space missions that successfully reach their planetary targets.

If the solar system has more than three planets, all affected by gravity, why is it not a major problem to predict their paths? Well, for the most part, the planets are all too far away from each other to affect each other's path very much. The planets' orbits are all mainly influenced by the Sun, which is very far away but so massive that it exerts a very powerful gravitational force. In some cases, however, planets do affect each other significantly. For example, the gravity of Neptune affects its neighbor Uranus in a small but visible way. In fact, Neptune was discovered as a planet only after scientists noticed its strange effects on the motion of Uranus.

as heavy as one another, each planet will cause the other to move in a visible way.

Think about two people running across a field toward each other and, when they get close, grabbing each other's arms. If the two people are both about the same size and weight, they will both swing around and fly off in different directions. But if the two people are father and child, the father will probably just scoop the child up in his arms and into the air. In more scientific language, objects that are close in mass will both influence the path of the other; if objects are very different in mass, the lighter one will probably not affect the path of the heavier one very much at all. Earlier scientists had realized that the Earth pulled on the apple, but not until Newton did they realize that the apple also pulled on the Earth.

Newton was also the first to understand that gravity worked throughout the universe and that the same gravity that pulled an apple to the Earth would pull a comet toward the Sun—or would pull the Moon toward the Earth. Then, one final revelation made everything fall into place.

It is reasonable to assume that the Earth's gravity will be weaker as an object moves farther from it. After all, a light looks dimmer when it is moved farther away, so scientists of the past thought that maybe gravity acted the same way. In 1679, prodded by a rival scientist (Robert Hooke), Newton was able to show that the force of gravity drops off with the inverse square of the distance between two objects. What does that mean? If one astronaut is twice as far from a planet as another astronaut, the force that the first astronaut feels from gravity will be ¼ as strong as the force felt by the second, closer astronaut, and if the first astronaut's spaceship moves three times as far away, the force of gravity will be $1/9$ as strong. When Newton put the **inverse square law** together with everything else, he found that he could explain the motion of everything in the universe. From throwing a ball to a friend, to shooting a rocket into space, to putting a satellite in orbit around the Earth, to understanding how Earth moves around the Sun—the motion of all of these things, and more, could be explained by the new laws of gravity.

It is hard to overstate just how important Newton's discoveries were, so here is one way to look at it. In Newton's day, scientists believed that some kinds of birds lived underwater during the winter; they had not realized that birds migrate south for the winter. People thought that fossils were simply strange patterns in the rocks; they did not understand that they were really the remains of ancient life. Many people thought that **meteors** were strange sparks in the night sky; they did not know that they were actually pieces of sand and rock from outer space entering the atmosphere. All of these ideas and hundreds more have been found to be false in the three centuries since Newton first developed his laws of gravity. All of these ideas have been superseded by newer, more accurate ideas. But when *Cassini* was launched toward Saturn, Newton's mathematics and Newton's physics were used to calculate the path that the spacecraft would use to cross the solar system, and Newton's work was used to make sure that the planet would be there when the spaceship arrived. Astronomers are still using Newton's discoveries to measure the motion of stars, galaxies, and everything else in the universe. Newton may have been a miserable and mean man, but he was a wonderful scientist, and he is justly recognized as one of the most brilliant people of all time.

In just over a century, humankind's understanding of the universe had changed profoundly. Copernicus had shown that the Earth circled the Sun, not the other way around. Galileo had shown that the Earth was just another object in space, special only in that it was our home. Kepler had shown that planets moved in orbits, and Halley showed that comets did as well. Thanks to all of them, scientists had learned that the universe was for the most part predictable, and that it followed certain rules. Thanks to Newton, Hooke, and Halley, and to the new language of mathematics that Newton helped to invent, scientists now knew how and why the planets did what they did; how and why they moved as they moved. Never before had scientific understanding of the universe come so far in so short a period of time, and it would be a few more centuries before anything like this happened again.

The Laws of
Planetary Motion

From the ancient Egyptians to the time of Newton, the planets that were first seen as gods ended up as objects in the universe subject to the same laws as a simple apple. The Earth moved from being the center of the universe to being just another planet. The study of planetary motion has transformed from simple observations to universal laws. So, now it is time to learn more about these laws—what they are and how they work. Now, there will be a little math in this chapter, but that is because (as Galileo said), math is the language of the universe. But the math is necessary to really understand what is going on. This branch of mathematics, which can actually get to be very complicated, is called **celestial mechanics**. Its development and use is one of the greatest intellectual triumphs in the history of science.

TYCHO BRAHE

Tycho Brahe was a phenomenally good observer of the skies, and he made it his mission to chart the location of every star he could see. He also made it a mission to learn as much as he could about the motions of the planets—Tycho wanted to try to understand exactly how they moved, and why.

Tycho lived during an interesting time in the history of science. Copernicus had shown that his model of the solar system (with all of the planets, including the Earth, orbiting the Sun) did a much better job of explaining the motions of the planets. In fact, the Copernican system was gaining more and more acceptance among the scientists of the day. At the same time, however, the church rejected any plan of the universe that did not have the Earth at the center. So, for a scientist like Tycho who was also a religious believer, things could be difficult—what his intellect told him and what the church told him were at odds with each other. Both could not be right.

Tycho was trying to reconcile these two opposing views—he wanted them *both* to be right. Tycho's scientific reasoning told him that Copernicus made sense. But Tycho also noticed that gravity pulled everything toward the Earth, and he assumed that the Earth pulled on the Sun, the Moon, the other planets, and the stars as well. If everything in the universe (as Tycho saw it) was being pulled toward the Earth, then the Earth simply *had* to be at the center of everything.

What Tycho came up with was a system in which the Earth remained at the center, but the rest of the planets circled the Sun, which itself orbited the Earth. Tycho wanted to find something that would satisfy both his intellect and his religious beliefs. Ultimately, his system did not stand the test of time, and it lasted only a little while. But what did remain from Tycho's work were some of the most amazingly precise measurements of planetary positions and motions that had been compiled up to that time. These measurements were vitally important to Tycho's student, Johannes Kepler.

JOHANNES KEPLER

Kepler was, without a doubt, Tycho's greatest student. Tycho collected the data, but Kepler was the one to start to figure out what it all meant.

It began when Tycho set Kepler to work on the orbit of Mars. Mars was one of the closest planets, and it should have been easy to figure out its orbit. Yet Mars could never be found at its predicted position, and Kepler wanted to know why. After a great deal of work, he finally figured it out—and came up with what is known as **Kepler's first law** of planetary motion at the same time.

Kepler's First Law

Johannes Kepler's first law of planetary motion is comprised of three central observations that, together, explain the apparent motion of the planets of the solar system.

Figure 4.1   Johannes Kepler devised three laws of planetary motion.

1. Planets move in ellipses with the Sun at one focus.

Copernicus's model of the solar system correctly had the Sun at the center, but Copernicus was convinced that the planets moved in perfect circles. But, as Tycho saw, Mars's actual position just did not fit with a circular orbit—sometimes it moved more quickly than it should, and sometimes it inexplicably slowed down. The problem was that real orbits are not perfect circles—Kepler found out that the actual orbits are **ellipses**. Ellipses are important enough to spend some time learning about.

Take a circle and stretch it a little bit and it becomes an ellipse. In a circle, every point on the circle is exactly the same distance from the center. In an ellipse, some points are closer and others are farther away. Every ellipse also has two foci (the singular form is "focus"), which are similar to the center of a circle. The way the foci work is like this: Picture cutting a circle out of a piece of rubber—maybe about 3 or 4 inches (8 or 10 cm) across. Now, pinch the center of the circle with both hands and pull. As the rubber stretches, the shape changes—it starts to stretch in one direction. It turns into an ellipse. In this ellipse, the foci are where the fingers are holding on to the

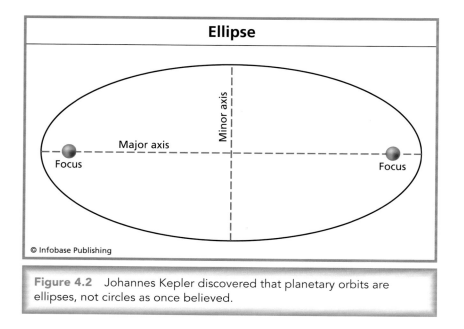

© Infobase Publishing

Figure 4.2   Johannes Kepler discovered that planetary orbits are ellipses, not circles as once believed.

rubber. If the fingers are closer together, it is more like a perfect circle. When it stretches a lot—when the fingers are far apart—it is a much more elongated ellipse. Basically, a circle is simply an ellipse with only one focus. The amount of stretching is called the eccentricity of the ellipse—a circle has an eccentricity of zero, and a highly stretched ellipse will have a high eccentricity, close to one. So, the smaller the degree of eccentricity, the closer it is to being a perfect circle.

What Kepler found was that planet's orbits are not perfect circles; they are ellipses. This was why Mars was not in its expected location—Tycho was expecting it to follow a circle.

2. The radius vector sweeps out equal areas in equal times.

This law is a bit more complicated, and it uses some terms that are not very obvious. So, it is helpful to understand each of the terms and then put it all together. Basically, what this law means is that a planet will move faster when it is close to the Sun and slower when it is far away. Let's see how.

The first term, *vector*, is like an arrow. It is a very special type of arrow—one that that points in a precise direction and has an exact length, or magnitude. The *radius* is a line that points from the center of a circle (or from one focus of an ellipse) to the *perimeter*, or outside edge, of the circle. So, in planetary motion, a radius vector is an arrow that begins at the Sun and ends at the planet. Now—this is an important point—the radius vector moves along with the planet. So, when the planet is farther from the Sun, the radius vector is longer than when the planet is closer to the Sun.

Next, consider a triangle. The area of a triangle is ½ times the length of its base times the height of the triangle. This is shown in Figure 4.3. In this picture, the height of the triangle is like the distance that the planet is from the Sun. The base of the triangle is how far the planet has moved in its orbit. Now, here is what Kepler might have meant in his second law.

First, the length of the radius vector can change—it depends on the planet's distance from the Sun. A planet in an elliptical orbit is sometimes closer and sometimes farther from the Sun. What Kepler is saying is that the area of this triangle—½ times the distance from the Sun times the length of the base, which is swept out by

The Law of Equal Areas

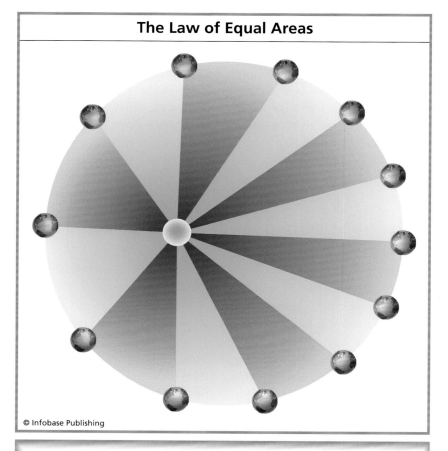

© Infobase Publishing

Figure 4.3   These triangles illustrate the law of equal areas. Though a planet might be farther away from the sun (the length of the triangle), as long as the distance it has moved in its orbit is the same (the base of the triangle), the area will be the same. A planet farther from the Sun is moving slower than when it is close to the Sun.

its orbit, stays the same for a planet no matter where it is in its orbit, over a given time interval—a day, a week, or a year. So, look at the drawing again, and think of it in terms of a planet orbiting the Sun. If the triangle on the left is the planet when it is closest and the triangle on the right is the planet when it is farthest from the Sun, **Kepler's second law** begins to make sense. *When the planet is* *farther from the Sun, the only way to make the areas the same size is to shorten the base of the longer triangle.* That means that a planet farther from the Sun is moving slower than one that is close to the Sun. So, this is what Kepler meant—when a planet is closer to the Sun (or when a moon is closer to a planet), it is moving faster than when it is far away. Just as important, it is possible to calculate how quickly a planet will be moving at any point in its orbit—all that needs to be known is how far it is from the Sun. Kepler was coming even closer to knowing why Mars was not where it was supposed to be.

In fact, Kepler's first two laws apply to any single planet as it moves along in its orbit, but they cannot compare planets in different orbits. Kepler could understand Mars, but he could not compare Mars to Jupiter or Venus. To do that, he had to go a bit further—to his third law.

3. The orbital period squared is proportional to the mean distance cubed.

Kepler's third law may sound like a lot of math—but it unlocks many secrets about the planets and moons in the solar system. By plugging in some information about the Earth, Kepler's third law can provide the distance of every other planet to the Sun, and the length of each planet's year.

Here is how it works. The orbital period, which Kepler called "periodic times," just means the amount of time it takes to complete a single orbit. For the Moon, the orbital period is about 28 days (the amount of time for the Moon to make a complete orbit around the Earth), and for the Earth, the orbital period is a year. So, that part is pretty easy. The math part is not too bad, either.

To square a number is to multiply it by itself. So, 5 squared—5^2—is 5 x 5, or 25. To cube a number means to multiply it by itself three times—so 2 cubed is 2 x 2 x 2 = 8. Or, in mathematical notation, $2^3 = 8$.

So, let's put this information into practice. Take Mars, for example. A year on Mars lasts for 687 days—that is how long it takes to make a complete orbit around the Sun. Compare this to Earth, which has a year of about 365 days. Also, Earth is about 93 million miles (150 million km) from the Sun, a distance called 1 astronomical unit. So, these bits of information can determine pre-cisely how far Mars is from the Earth.

Kepler's third law says to divide the square of the length of Mars's year (687 days x 687 days) by the square of Earth's year (365 days x 365 days), and then multiply this by the distance from the Earth to the Sun (93 million miles). It might be easier to see this in an equation.

$$P^2 \propto r^3 \quad (\propto \text{ means "is proportional to")}$$

$$\frac{P_M^2}{P_E^2} = \frac{r_M^3}{r_E^3} \quad \text{so} \quad \frac{P_M^2}{P_E^2} \times r_E^3 = r_M^3$$

$$\text{So:} \quad r_M^3 = \frac{687^2}{365^2} \times 1\text{AU}^3 = \frac{471{,}969}{133{,}225} \times 1 = 3.54$$

And, finally: $\sqrt[3]{3.54} = 1.52$

Here, P is the time to make a full orbit (the length of the year) and r is the distance to the Sun (the radius). So, by Kepler's laws, the cube of Mars's distance to the Sun (compared to the Earth's) is 3.54, which is the cube of 1.52 (remember, this means that 1.52 x 1.52 x 1.52 = 3.54). So, Kepler's third law says that Mars should be about 1.52 times as far from the Sun as the Earth is. That is, it should orbit at a distance of 1.52 astronomical units, or 1.52 AU from the Sun. As it turns out, Mars is, indeed, exactly where Kepler said it should be—right at 1.52 AU. In fact, every planet and moon in the solar system obeys Kepler's law almost perfectly. Kepler had learned something very important about the way that the solar system works.

So—Kepler's first law states that planets' orbits are ellipses, with the Sun at one focus. His second law says that planets (and comets, and anything else in space) move faster when they are closer to the Sun (or whatever they are orbiting), and Kepler's third law shows how to determine how far a planet is from the Sun, if we know how long the orbit takes. Kepler's laws demonstrate how to calculate a planet's orbit—how to tell where it will be in space—but he still did not really understand why the universe works this way. That is where Newton comes in.

ISAAC NEWTON

Newton knew *how* the planets moved through space, but he wanted to figure out *why* they moved that way. Another way to look at it is that Kepler showed that planetary orbits are ellipses, but he could not explain why a circle would not work just as well.

First, it is important to understand why the "why" part of this was so important to Newton. Imagine a cook is preparing dinner— he is making spaghetti, and he is boiling water to cook the noodles and simmering the sauce on the stove. There are some dials at the front of the stove. The dial for the burner underneath the sauce is turned so that the letter L is lined up with a small arrow outside the dial. The dial for the burner beneath the water is set to H.

Now, if spaghetti is all he really wants to cook, this is all that he needs to know about working the stove—he boils water on H and he heats the sauce on L. To him, it does not matter what H and L mean; all he needs to know is that H boils and L heats. But what if he wants to make something else? What if he is trying to cook pancakes for breakfast? If he uses L, the pancakes will never cook, and on H, they will burn. He needs to know more—a lot more. He needs to realize, for example, that H means "high heat" and L means "low heat." Knowing that, he can guess that all of the numbers in between are for different levels of heat between low and high—maybe one of these is good for pancakes. Of course, he also needs to know how to mix the pancake batter, he has to understand to flip the pancakes (and when), and he has to know when they are finished. In fact, he needs to have a whole theory of pancake making and a theory of stove operating in order to make his breakfast. If he wants to be able to make hot dogs, tuna-noodle casserole, and other dishes, he actually needs to come up with a theory of cooking.

Likewise, Kepler noticed how the planets moved, but his observations and his theories were limited to just those planets, and not other systems: not for the moons of Mars, the moons of Jupiter and Saturn, or for anything else. In effect, Kepler had learned how to cook spaghetti, but was not quite sure how to make pancakes—or anything else. That is not to say Kepler was not smart—learning what he did was an incredible achievement, and that is why professors still talk about him today. But his work applied only to what he could see at the time; there was no way to understand why it worked, or even if it would work elsewhere in the universe. Those were the things that Newton wanted to learn.

One place to start was with regular motion—maybe a planet moving through space was just like a ball or a bullet moving through the air. So, Newton tried to understand how objects move, and he came up with three laws of his own.

Newton's Laws of Motion

1. Every object in a state of uniform motion tends to remain in that state of motion unless an external force is applied to it.

Newton's first law simply says that nothing changes its speed or its direction unless it is pulled or pushed. For example, a ball sitting on the floor keeps sitting on the floor unless someone pushes it. Once pushed, it keeps going until something (like friction with the floor, or the resistance of the air) brings it to a stop. Gravity is a force, too. So, tilting a flat board containing a ball rolls the ball because gravity pulls it down.

2. The relationship between an object's mass, m, its acceleration, a, and the applied force, F, is F = ma.

What **Newton's second law** says is that pushing something harder speeds it up, or accelerates it. It also says that the same amount of force—the same push—will move a light object faster than it will move a heavy object. So, if a child playfully pushes a parent on a swing, the parent will not move very far, but if the parent gives a child's swing a push, the child ends up going much higher.

3. For every action there is an equal and opposite reaction.

This law is also about pushing. Here, Newton is saying that when an older brother tries to push a younger brother, the younger brother will move in the opposite direction as the older brother. If the younger brother stands on ice and gives the older brother a push, the older brother will move in one direction and the younger brother will slide back a little bit, too—this is the "action-reaction" that Newton is talking about. This is how jet airplanes move and how rockets leave the Earth's atmosphere. In space, there is nothing for the rocket exhaust to push against, so it works a bit differently. But if exhaust gas comes out of one end of the rocket, the rocket will move in the other direction, just as when a person falls off a skateboard—the person may fall forward, and the skateboard will roll backward.

So, here is how Newton's laws apply to the motion of planets.

According to Newton's first law, planets should move at a constant speed and in a straight line unless there is something pulling or pushing on them. But this is not what planets do—planets move in a circle, speed up, and slow down in their orbits. So, something has to be pushing or pulling on them. What is pulling on the planets? What forces them to move in elliptical orbits?

According to Newton's second law, the amount of force on a planet—what is causing it to speed up, slow down, or move in a curved orbit—depends on where the planet is in the solar system. For example, a planet in a distant orbit has a path that curves only a very little bit compared to a planet with a very small orbit. So, this force in the outer solar system must be much weaker than the force in the inner solar system. But why? And how much weaker is it?

According to **Newton's third law**, if something forces a planet to change its path—if something is acting as a force on the planet—then the planet should be exerting a force, too. The planet pulls on everything that is pulling on it. So, what does this mean for the way the solar system works?

The answers to some of these questions were already known. For years, it was assumed that gravity was the force pulling on the planets. It was known that the force of gravity could bend a planet's path from a straight line into a circle—this is something that can be proved right here on Earth. Think of throwing a ball forward. The ball will fly straight away for a short distance, and then it curves down and falls to the ground. It is curving because gravity is pulling it to the ground. Any object thrown in the air will follow a similar path. So, this is part of the answer for why planets follow orbits—the gravity from the Sun pulls them around from a straight line into a curve. But planets, moons, and satellites go around forever, and a

Newton's Cannonball

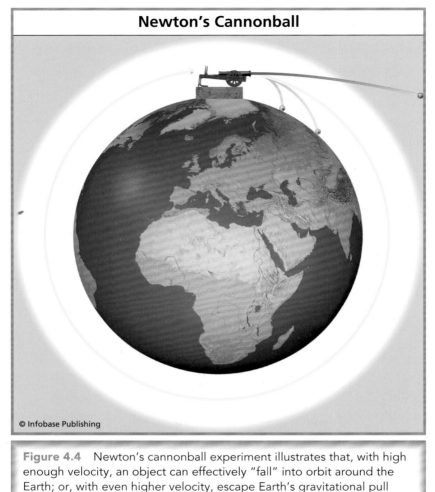

Figure 4.4   Newton's cannonball experiment illustrates that, with high enough velocity, an object can effectively "fall" into orbit around the Earth; or, with even higher velocity, escape Earth's gravitational pull entirely.

ball falls to the ground fairly quickly—there is still something happening here.

The answer to this is actually not very difficult—imagine throwing a ball faster and faster. The ball will travel farther and farther. If it travels farther, the Earth begins to curve away from it because the Earth is round. Shooting a ball really, *really* hard might make it go all the way around the Earth before it finally falls to the ground. Shoot it even faster, and it will keep falling around the Earth forever. At that point, the ball is in orbit. The ball is trying to fly in a straight line, but the force of gravity is pulling it into a curve. The surface of the Earth is curved, too, and if the ball is moving fast enough and far enough, its curved path will be larger than the curve of the Earth. So, the ball keeps falling around the Earth forever—in exactly the same way that the Moon falls around the Earth forever, and the planets fall around the Sun forever. In fact, a satellite can orbit an object of any shape, and the exact path of the orbit will depend on the shape of the object being orbited. Even the Earth is not a perfect sphere, and the orbits of satellites are not perfectly round; they dip and bend very slightly as they pass over parts of the Earth that are more or less massive and that vary from perfect roundness.

So, Newton's first law helps to explain why the planets orbit the Sun, but not why the orbits are elliptical.

Newton was not the only one thinking about these things— many of the smartest people of that time were trying to figure out planetary motions. One of them, a rival of Newton's named Robert Hooke, even wrote a letter to Newton in 1679, asking Newton's opinion on one theory. Hooke thought that, if the Sun's gravity got weaker as planets got farther away from it, this could explain why planets have elliptical orbits. This was an important question—and Newton never replied to Hooke, for reasons that may never become completely clear.

In 1672, a French scientist named Jean Richer showed that pendulums swing more slowly at the Earth's equator than they do closer to the poles. Newton proved that this was because the Earth is not a perfect sphere—it bulges out at the equator, so the equator is farther from the center of the Earth than the poles. He also showed that gravity is weaker at a greater distance—this is the inverse relationship that Hooke was talking about. The force of gravity is weaker at a greater distance. But this was on Earth—would it work across the solar system, too? And how much weaker was gravity at a distance? Was it a little bit weaker, or a lot?

Hooke proposed that the Sun's gravity on the planets dropped off inversely with distance. This means that, if one planet is twice as far from the Sun as another planet, the Sun's gravity on the farther planet is half as strong. At three times the distance, gravity would be one-third as strong, and so forth. So, at Mars (which is 1.52 times as far from the Sun as is the Earth), the Sun should pull only about two-thirds as strongly as it does on the Earth—if Hooke was correct.

When Hooke did not hear back from Newton, he began telling his friends that he had finally solved the problem of planetary motion. This upset Newton, who did not like Hooke very much at all. So, Newton decided to see if Hooke was correct, and in 1680, he found that Hooke had made a very important mistake—the force of gravity did, indeed, drop with distance, but it dropped with the *square* of the distance. This is called the inverse square law, and it turns out that it describes many phenomena besides gravity.

The inverse square law says that moving twice as far from the Sun does not drop gravity by a factor of 2, but by a factor of 2^2. This is a huge difference—the difference between ½ and ¼ of the original gravity. The difference only gets larger as the distance grows. Under Hooke's inverse relationship, Jupiter (at a distance of 5.2 AU) would experience $1/5$ the force of gravity, while Newton correctly calculated it would actually only see $1/25$ of the gravitational pull that the Earth experiences. As he went through his calculations, Newton also saw how an inverse square law perfectly explained the planets' orbits.

This was a major discovery, and Newton rushed right out to say . . . nothing. For some reason, Newton finished his calculations, and then just sat on his results. He was happy to have solved the problem, but he did not seem to care if anyone else knew or not. In fact, it was not until 1684 that Newton said anything to anyone, and another two years would pass before he got around to writing up his results and publishing them in a book, *Principia de Motu Corporum* (the Principles of the Motion of Bodies) so that other scientists could see what he had done. The expanded version of this book, known today as the *Principia Mathematica*, is considered one of the greatest works of science ever written, along with Newton's books on optics and mathematics and Darwin's book on evolution.

But wait—there is more. Newton also realized that the force of gravity is related to the mass of the objects. A massive planet has stronger gravity than a light planet. So, Newton's full law of gravity looks like this:

$$F = \frac{GMm}{r^2}$$

In this equation, F is the force of gravity, M is the mass of one object (the Earth, for example), m is the mass of the other object (such as the Moon), and r is the distance between them. The other term, G, is called Newton's gravitational constant—it is one of many **physical constants** that scientists use to help understand the universe. By knowing how massive each object is, how far apart they are, and what G is, it is possible to find out how much they pull on each other. So, Newton's law can determine how much gravitational force there is between the Earth and the Moon. It can tell scientists how quickly a black hole will pull a star to its doom. It can also show how much gravitational force a planet exerts on a spacecraft. Newton's law is what the *Cassini* navigational team used to calculate not only where the planets would be, but how the gravity of each planet would affect the spacecraft. Amazingly, this theory was developed more than 300 years ago.

But the best is yet to come. Newton called his law the **law of universal gravitation**, and the "universal" part is important. Newton was not saying that this is how the Moon works, or even how the solar system works; he was saying that this is how the *universe* works—the whole thing. When astronomers look at stars in the Milky Way galaxy, they use Newton's laws to describe their motion. When astrophysicists discover new planets circling other stars, they again can use Newton's laws to calculate how big the planet is (the planet's mass is the *m* in his equation). Newton's laws still work, and they have been working exactly the same way for the billions of years since the universe first formed. The fact that they can be used to describe parts of the universe that Newton could not even imagine, and at distances (and for times) that he could not conceive of, is equally amazing.

Newton was certainly one of the most brilliant scientists in history, and he deserves all of the respect we can give him. Yet as brilliant as he was, Newton still did not explain exactly what gravity is, and there were still a few loose ends to tidy up. Nevertheless, for 200 years, nobody saw a need to try to improve on his work—until Albert Einstein came along.

What Is a Physical Constant?

Scientists use mathematical equations to describe the way that the universe works. Many of these equations contain what are called physical constants—like the G in Newton's law of gravitation. Physical constants provide the key to a lot of important information about the universe.

There are actually a few different kinds of physical constants. Some are measurements, like the mass of the electron or the speed of light. This sort of physical constant is simply how much something weighs, how large it is, or how quickly it moves in specific measurement units (for example, in miles per hour or in grams). So, for example, a chart can list how many grams an electron is, or the radius of a proton in centimeters. These numbers are very small, but as far as scientists know, these measurements never change. The astronomical unit, which was mentioned earlier, is another physical constant.

Another sort of physical constant is like Newton's gravitational constant. These constants help mathematical equations, using measurement units, to describe the universe. It is important to remember that the units we use on Earth—pounds, kilograms, meters, feet, seconds, and so forth—are unique to this planet. One kilogram, for example, was originally defined as being the mass of 1 liter of water, and 1 liter is the volume of 1,000 cubic centimeters. But these are measurements that humans on Earth developed, and the universe does not know (or care) how people measure mass, length, or time. So, when Newton wrote his equation, he was using his units, and he developed a

ALBERT EINSTEIN

As good as Newton's work was, it still did not explain everything. For example, even though scientists knew how gravity worked, nobody

factor—a physical constant—so that the answer to his calculations was something that could be understood by other scientists on Earth. One can imagine that inhabitants of another planet might have come up with a different system of units to measure things.

There are dozens of physical constants that scientists have discovered, measured, or calculated. Here are some of them.

Physical constant and symbol	Value and units	What it means
Speed of light in a vacuum (c)	299,792,458 meters per second	This is how fast light travels when there is nothing in its way—the universe's ultimate speed limit.
Newton's gravitational constant (G)	$6.67428(67) \times 10^{-11}\,m^3/\,kg{\cdot}s^2$	This helps to calculate the force that gravity exerts on an object.
Electron mass (m_e)	$9.109\,382\,15(45) \times 10^{-31}$ kg	The mass of an electron
Gravitational acceleration (g)	$9.80665\,m/\,sec^2$	How quickly falling objects on Earth accelerate

really knew what gravity *was*. Then there was Mercury, the closest planet to the Sun. For some reason, Newton's laws did not seem to work for Mercury. Its orbit seemed to shift over time, and nobody could quite understand why.

If Newton was the greatest scientist of his time, then Einstein must certainly go down as the greatest scientist of the modern world, and Einstein's accomplishments are just as important as Newton's. Though Einstein made many amazing accomplishments in science, this book will cover just one—his work on gravity.

Newton thought of gravity as being some force that worked between two objects—like a rubber band that pulls the two objects toward each other. Einstein thought about things a little differently—he did not like the idea of rubber bands, even imaginary ones. What Einstein did, instead, was to try to get a picture in his mind of what space itself might look like.

One image that comes to mind is a rubber sheet, and each planet is like a marble sitting on the sheet. Massive planets make deeper dents in the sheet; small, light planets make shallow dents.

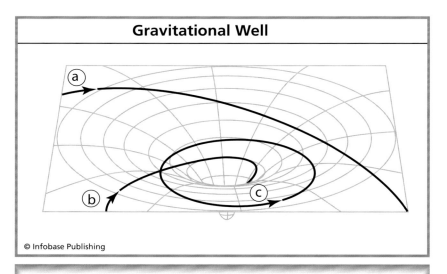

Gravitational Well

© Infobase Publishing

Figure 4.5 A rubber-sheet model of gravitation according to the general theory of relativity. A heavy object, such as a marble, placed on a stretched horizonal rubber sheet, deforms the sheet, just as a massive object deforms the "fabric" of space. This image represents the orbit of an object in space and the letters show spots of friction, which cause the object to drop down to a lower orbit.

Approaching a planet is like descending more and more steeply into a valley. In Einstein's theory, a steeper slope means stronger gravity. The steepness of the slope indicates the strength of the gravitational field. To paint another picture, it is harder and takes greater force to push a wheelbarrow up a steep hill compared to a flat surface. In effect, Einstein showed that gravity is simply due to the effects of planets and stars on the shape of space.

Weight Versus Mass

Everyone is used to the word *weight*; weight is what people see when they step on the scale and when they weigh fruit at the grocery store. But what someone calls "weight" is actually a bit more complicated than this. Weight, in fact, can change from place to place because, in reality, weight depends on the strength of the pull of gravity in a particular place.

To a scientist, weight is actually the mass of an object multiplied by the pull of gravity. As the strength of gravity changes, the weight also changes. So, an object that has a given mass (which does not change) will weigh more on Earth than on the Moon, and it will weigh less on the Moon than on Mars. Even on Earth, the weight of an object will change very slightly from place to place—the top of a mountain, for example, is farther from the center of the Earth than the bottom of the ocean, so the same object will weigh just a little more on a mountaintop than it will on the seafloor, because the force of gravity is just a little lower at high elevations. So, everyone's mass is the same everywhere in the universe, but their weight will change if they go from one planet to another, or even one altitude to another on Earth.

There are actually two kinds of mass. An object's **inertial mass** determines how much an object will accelerate when it is pushed or pulled by a fixed amount of force—

(continues)

(continued)

this is the mass in Newton's second law, $F = ma$. **Gravitational mass** determines how much an object will accelerate when another object (such as the Earth) exerts the force of gravity on it—this is the mass in Newton's law of universal gravitation.

An object's inertial mass always equals its gravitational mass. This is strange, because the two do not have to be the same. This would have been a mystery to Newton. However, Einstein figured out why they are the same. It goes like this: Imagine a person inside a moving elevator, without knowing what is outside. If the person drops a ball in the elevator, the ball would drop in the same way whether the elevator is on the Earth (which would accelerate the ball to the ground due to gravity) or in zero gravity space, inside a rocket ship accelerating upward by an amount equal to the acceleration due to Earth's gravity. From this insight, that an accelerating rocket in zero-gravity space could provide the same conditions as a gravitational field, Einstein developed his general theory of relativity, which provides the modern understanding of gravity.

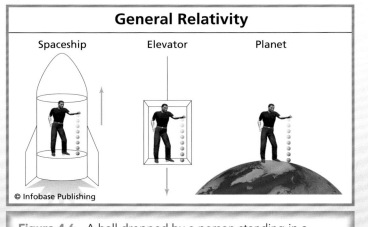

General Relativity

Spaceship   Elevator   Planet

© Infobase Publishing

Figure 4.6 A ball dropped by a person standing in a launching rocket ship, a moving elevator, or on stationary ground, would fall at the same rate. Its perceived speed depends on the frame of reference of the viewer.

What this has to do with Mercury is even more interesting. It turns out that as the Sun rotates, it drags space around with it, and Mercury gets caught up in that. The next time someone makes pancakes (or even a cake), here is a short experiment to do. Put a wooden spoon into the pancake (or cake) batter and start to spin it. What will happen is that the batter closest to the handle of the spoon will twist a little bit, too—not as quickly as the spoon, but faster than the batter a little farther out. If there is a small bubble in the batter, it will be pulled around, too—not as fast as the spoon, but it will be noticeable. This is what is happening to Mercury—as the Sun spins in space, it drags space along with it a little bit, and Mercury is caught up with the space as it twists. The result is that Mercury's point of closest approach to the Sun shifts very slightly. This shift is called precession. Newton's theory could not explain the amount of this shift, but Einstein's can. In fact, this happens around the Earth, too. A very recent experiment, called *Gravity Probe B*, put a satellite into orbit. The satellite contains three metal balls that are the most precisely machined things that have ever been made. Scientists found that after a few years in orbit, the metal balls had twisted ever so slightly—just what was expected from the Earth's rotation. It is not that Newton made a mistake; it is just that Einstein had the advantage of two extra centuries and a lot of progress.

5

More Than
Just Planets

The great thing about Newton's laws of planetary motion is that they do not just apply to planets—they apply to everything in the solar system.

KILLER ASTEROIDS

Sixty-five million years ago, a rock the size of a small city slammed into the Earth, somewhere around where the Yucatan Peninsula in Mexico is today. Moving at tens of miles every second, it took only a few seconds to pass through the entire atmosphere. At that speed, it hit the Earth with the force of millions of atomic bombs. Debris spread over the entire world, clouds of dust and smoke blocked the Sun, and fires burned for thousands of miles around the impact site. Today, the remnants of the crater are over 100 miles (161 km) in diameter, and traces of the asteroid can still be seen in certain layers of rock. Before the asteroid hit, dinosaurs were the major form of life on Earth and mammals were mostly insignificant. Afterward, the dinosaurs died out and mammals—eventually including humans—became dominant. A single, relatively small asteroid changed the world.

Figure 5.1 These fallen trees show some of the destruction of the Tunguska event in Russia.

On June 30, 1908, sometime around 7:00 or 8:00 in the morning, many Russians saw a fireball in the sky and heard a tremendous explosion. Years later, when scientists were finally able to visit the area, they found that more than 75 million trees had been knocked down, and they found evidence of a giant explosion. Scientists now estimate the explosion was about the strength of the largest nuclear weapon that has ever been detonated. The rock that caused all of this was probably about 60 to 70 feet (18 to 21 m) across.

The Earth lives in a dangerous neighborhood. Every part of the Moon is pockmarked with craters, and most of Mercury is heavily cratered, as is Mars. Evidence of past impacts is abundant on Earth, and even Venus—thick atmosphere and all—contains nearly 1,000 craters. The same is true in the outer solar system; the gas giants do not show craters, but that does not mean that they do not get hit by them, and every known moon has shown signs of impacts. In 1994, multiple fragments of Comet Shoemaker-Levy 9 hit Jupiter so hard that its effects could be seen from Earth. Killer asteroids have hit the Earth repeatedly, as they have hit every object in the solar system, and they will continue to do so as long as the Earth is around. A large object striking the Earth could kill millions of people, and that's if we are lucky.

There are as many as 1,000 asteroids that are large enough to cause serious damage whose orbits cross the Earth's. Every year or so, it seems, there is a news story about an asteroid that has passed (or will pass) perilously close to this planet. Again—this is a dangerous neighborhood; scientists are trying to find out exactly how dangerous it might be.

One of the things that makes it difficult to determine exactly how much risk the planet faces is that asteroid orbits are so complicated. Say, for example, that an asteroid is in space and its orbit takes it past the Earth. The Earth pulls the asteroid closer toward it. When the asteroid gets even closer, the Moon's gravity pulls on it as well. If it is complicated to figure out the forces of gravity on three objects, imagine calculating the effects of gravity on four bodies—the Earth, the Moon, the asteroid, and the Sun. But it gets even worse.

As the asteroid shoots past the Earth and Moon, it travels back toward the outer solar system. On the way, the asteroid will be pulled on by the gravity of Mars and, if it gets close enough, by Jupiter. These outer planets also change its orbit, making it even more difficult to figure out where it will be at any time in the future.

In fact, Jupiter plays a major role in the solar system. As the most massive planet, it has the strongest gravity; it pulls harder on other objects, and its pull reaches farther across space. In the early days of the solar system, Jupiter likely helped to protect the inner planets by helping to shepherd the asteroids into the region of space between it and Mars. Rocks hurtling from the outer solar system toward Earth's orbit might be deflected by Jupiter's gravity into an orbit that was less likely to strike the Earth. But now, with most of the asteroids in fairly stable orbit, Jupiter can also play the spoiler—nudging an asteroid from its orbit and sending it toward Earth. Most of the time they miss. Sometimes they do not.

On December 22, 2005, the U.S. Congress passed a law setting up a Near-Earth Object Survey program; its purpose is to "detect, track, catalogue, and characterize certain near-earth asteroids and comets." The goal is to watch everything in space that could possibly crash into the planet and cause casualties, so that humans can try to alter the orbit of these objects and save civilization from destruction. There are many strategies that are being studied, but the very first step must be to locate an asteroid and to use scientists' understand-

Migrating Planets?

It is easy to assume that the solar system looks the same today as it did billions of years ago. It is surprising to find out that this is not the case—some of the planets have actually changed their orbits, and they will keep doing this in the future.

One of the reasons for this is that the Sun is getting lighter; it is losing mass all the time because it is blowing out massive amounts of hydrogen every year—this and other debris from the Sun is called the **solar wind**. The Sun has lost as much as 20% of its original mass since it first formed, although much of this mass loss occurred before there were any planets. But over time, the Sun will continue very slowly to lose mass, and this will affect the planets a little bit.

As the Sun loses mass, its gravitational force drops slightly. With less gravitational force, the planets are going to move a little farther away from the Sun. With time, all of the planets will be moving away from the Sun ever so slightly.

But that is not all. Early in the history of the solar system, there was a lot of extra gas and dust. There has always been more gas and dust farther out from the Sun. As

(continues)

(continued)

the planets go around in their orbits, they transfer energy to the dust and gas. The gas and dust speed up a little, and the planets slow down slightly. Over millions of years, due to this braking action, the planets move a little closer to the Sun. Having said that, there is still a great deal that scientists do not know about this process, and a lot of exciting research is still going on in this area.

Early in the history of the solar system, it is possible that the planets migrated toward the Sun (although it is also possible for young planets to move away from their star as well). In the 4 billion years since that time, the loss of mass from the Sun has weakened its pull, and the planets have been moving back outward.

Planetary migrations happen in other solar systems as well. Outside of the solar system, scientists have located a lot of huge planets that are very close to their stars. In these solar systems, a planet the size of Jupiter is about as close to its parent star as Mercury is to the Sun, or even closer. When these "hot Jupiters" were first found, many astronomers did not believe it; there did not seem to be any way that a gas giant could form so close to a star. Astronomers finally realized that they did not form there; instead, these huge planets formed far from their stars, just as Jupiter and Saturn did. Over time, due to interaction with the dust and gas in the system, the planets gradually spiraled in toward their stars, ending up in an orbit that, at first, seemed impossible.

ing of planetary motion to see if it is a threat. If so, humans may be able to find a way to prevent objects in the solar system from causing harm.

So, what is the best thing to do if an asteroid heads toward Earth? Blow it up? Wait and hope?

Well, blowing up an asteroid is probably not an option—even the strongest nuclear weapons are not going to do any more than just dent an asteroid. At best, it will not change anything. At worst, the asteroid would break up into a lot of smaller fragments, each of which will hit the Earth.

Another idea is to put a small rocket motor on the asteroid. This strategy would take advantage of Newton's third law—the law that every action has an opposite reaction. If a small rocket motor is attached to the asteroid, the reaction will push the asteroid in the opposite direction—changing its orbit ever so slightly, but enough to miss the Earth.

Another idea is to put a spacecraft near the asteroid, holding a steady position on one side of the asteroid. This uses Newton's law of universal gravitation—even though the spacecraft is small, it will exert a tiny gravitational pull on the asteroid. If there is enough time, over a period of years, the gravity of the spacecraft will pull the asteroid enough to one side to cause it to miss the Earth. It does not have move to the other side of the solar system—just far enough to miss our planet. After that, it could be thousands of years before the asteroid is a threat again, and by then future scientists and engineers may be able to come up with an even better solution.

THE OORT CLOUD

Moving into the far outer reaches of the solar system, out beyond Neptune and Pluto, is the cold and icy wilderness—filled with all of the construction debris left over from the solar system's birth. Out here, anywhere from 50 to 50,000 times the distance between the Earth and the Sun (50 to 50,000 AU), the Sun's pull is a tiny fraction of what the Earth feels (the strongest pull there is $1/2{,}500$ as strong as at the Earth's orbit, and it get much weaker from there). This part of the solar system is called the **Oort cloud**, named for the great Dutch astronomer, Jan Oort, who first predicted its existence. It is cold out here, close to absolute zero (-459.67°F, or -273.15°C). The Oort cloud is full of comets—giant lumps of ice with a little bit of dust. What is out here is trillions of dirty snowballs. That's right—trillions.

Whatever is out here, according to Kepler's and Newton's laws, is going to be moving slowly. A light-year away from Earth and a quarter of the way to the nearest star, objects in the Oort cloud are

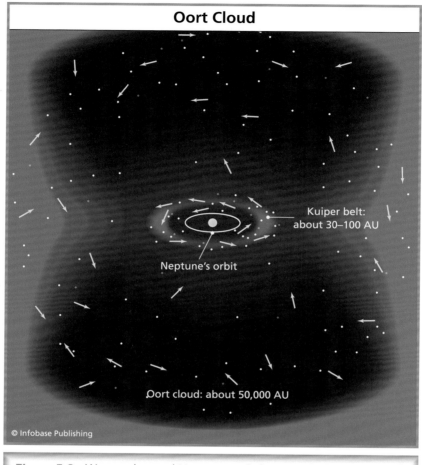

Oort Cloud

Kuiper belt:
about 30–100 AU

Neptune's orbit

Oort cloud: about 50,000 AU

© Infobase Publishing

Figure 5.2 Way out beyond Neptune and Pluto is the cold, icy region known as the Oort cloud, filled with debris from the solar system's birth.

drifting slowly through space, like bits of dust falling slowly through the air.

Normally, people do not worry about the Oort cloud. The comets there are so far from the Sun that they are barely tied by the Sun's gravity, and they are easy to knock out of their paths. In fact, this can happen—a passing star can rattle the Oort cloud, scattering comets the same way the wind from a passing car can scatter leaves next to the road (this is not to say that the star has to pass through the Oort cloud—remember how far away gravity can exert an effect). Some of these scattered comets will leave the solar system, and some will be sent inward. Thousands of years later,

Finding Neptune

Less than 100 years after Newton published his theories of gravitation and motion, astronomers used Newton's laws and Kepler's celestial mechanics to check their observations of Uranus's motion against their predictions. Instead of confirming Newton, these observations showed discrepancies that worsened with time. The dilemma was that either Newton's laws were incorrect or some force was pulling Uranus from its predicted path. Even taking into account the gravity of other major planets failed to fix this problem. The only other explanation was that there was another planet, even farther from the Sun than Uranus. Finally, in 1846, two mathematicians, Urbain Leverrier of France and John Adams of England, nearly simultaneously determined that another planet must be causing these deviations.

Both Leverrier and Adams had difficulty persuading their colleagues to search for the new planet. Adams ran into opposition from Sir George Airy, the astronomer royal of Great Britain, who just did not believe it was possible to discover a planet simply by performing mathematical calculations. Finally, Leverrier persuaded Johann Galle, a German astronomer, to search for the new planet. In England, Professor James Challis also agreed to try to find it. Aided by a set of new and unpublished star charts of the ecliptic (the plane in which the planets lie), Galle and his assistant Heinrich d'Arrest found the new planet in less than an hour on their first night of observations.

Of Leverrier's part in this discovery, the reigning French astronomer, François Arago, said: "In the eyes of all

(continues)

(continued)

impartial men, this discovery will remain one of the most magnificent triumphs of theoretical astronomy, one of the glories of the Académie and one of the most beautiful distinctions of our country."

Another of Leverrier's colleagues proclaimed: "He discovered a star with his pen, without any instruments other than the strength of his calculations alone."

What is interesting is that both Leverrier's and Adams's solutions for Neptune's orbit were wrong. They both assumed that Neptune was farther from the Sun than it actually is, leading in turn to flawed calculations of Neptune's actual orbit. In fact, while the calculated position was correct, had the search taken place even a year earlier or later, Neptune would not have been discovered so readily, and both Leverrier and Adams might well be unknown today except as obscure historical footnotes. According to one writer, "Leverrier's planet in the end matched neither the orbit, size, location nor any other significant characteristic of the planet Neptune, but he still garners most of the credit for discovering it."

Astronomers also found out that Neptune's mass and orbital path are actually insufficient to account for all of the discrepancies in Uranus's motion. Not only that, but Neptune appeared to have discrepancies in *its* orbit. This spurred even more searches that ended with Pluto's discovery in 1930. However, since Pluto is not large enough to cause Neptune and Uranus to diverge from their orbits, some astronomers are wondering if there are even more planets beyond Pluto. In reality, along with the many years of hard work scanning the skies by Clyde Tombaugh, Pluto's discovery seems to be due more to remarkable coincidence than to an understanding of the physics of planetary motion. Recent studies suggest that these orbital discrepancies do not actually exist and are due, instead, to plotting the planets' positions on the poor star charts that existed until just recently.

the comet will swing past Jupiter and enter the inner solar system, maybe appearing in the sky spouting a beautiful tail—and maybe headed our way.

6

Other Solar Systems

According to the ancient Greek philosophers Thales and Anaximander, there was no doubt: An infinite universe must contain other worlds, and some of these other worlds must have life on them. There are thousands of other worlds, according to the Talmud, a set of writings in the Jewish religion from more than 1,500 years ago. Some medieval Jewish scholars even tried to think about what life on these other worlds might look like. In Islam, Allah, or God, is the Lord of all the worlds, and the Koran has some passages that can be interpreted to refer to other planets and their inhabitants. (Sadly, the Catholic Church has strongly disagreed in the past; when Giordano Bruno stated in the sixteenth century that the universe was infinite and that other stars were circled by other planets, he was executed for heresy.) The idea that there might be worlds other than the Earth is an ancient idea, and an idea that convinced more and more scientists after the telescope was invented.

At the time Galileo first looked through his telescope, the **Ptolemaic universe**, in which everything revolved around the Earth, was accepted as true by the Catholic Church. When people thought about it at all, they found it natural to assume that what they saw in the skies was the literal truth; they saw the stars turning through the sky. They did not think of a turning Earth; after all, if the Earth turned, why did they not feel the motion? Instead, they thought of a stationary Earth and a spinning universe. The thinking went that if everything spun around with the Earth at the center, there could be no thought of other planets around other stars.

The telescope changed all of this. Galileo saw, with his own eyes, that Jupiter had its own moons; that the moons orbited Jupiter and not the Earth. Jupiter was the center of its own system of worlds. Then, looking at the Milky Way, Galileo saw too many stars to count; he was perhaps the first person to understand the countless number of stars in the skies. His discoveries helped others to believe that there had to be even more to the universe than any person could see. In such a large place, with so many previously invisible stars, surely there were also planets out there that people could not yet see. That was the problem—no matter what scientists imagined, they just could not see something as small and dim as a planet around another star. In fact, until just 50 years ago, scientists could barely see Pluto, and that is in this solar system!

In 1855, Captain W.S. Jacob, observing stars from Madras, reported that he was certain he had found evidence of a planet circling the double star 70 Ophiuchi. Forty years later, the University of Chicago's Thomas See (who also observed at the U.S. Naval Observatory) agreed and suggested that this planet completed its trip around the stars every 36 years. Neither man actually saw a planet through his telescope; what they saw was the star wiggling back and forth, apparently tugged to and fro by the gravity of the circling planet. (Remember Newton's law of gravitation?) Unfortunately, it did not take very long for Forest Moulton (another American astronomer) to show that such an orbit would not make sense according to the laws of physics and that therefore such a planet could not exist. Sometime later, in the 1950s and 1960s, Swarthmore College professor Peter van der Kamp announced finding evidence of planets circling Barnard's Star, just six light-years from the Sun, but these were also later shown to be false.

So, what was the problem? Well, these astronomers were not stupid, and they were not making dumb mistakes. The problem is that, even today, scientists can barely see something the size of a planet so far away, even using the best telescopes, the best computers, and the best technology available. Even today, we can only "see" planets around very tiny, dim stars called brown dwarfs.

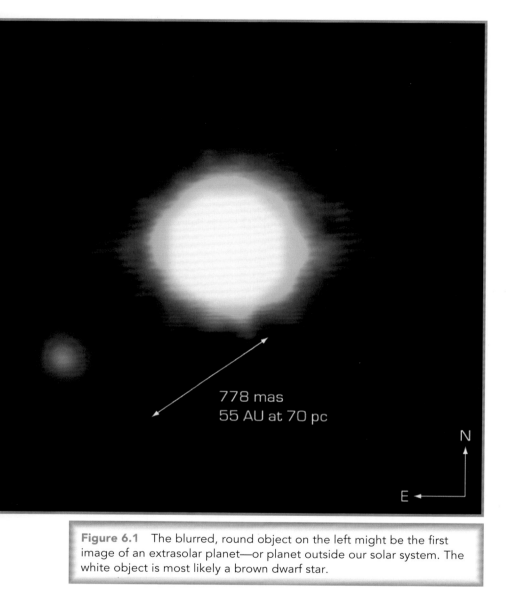

778 mas
55 AU at 70 pc

N

E

Figure 6.1 The blurred, round object on the left might be the first image of an extrasolar planet—or planet outside our solar system. The white object is most likely a brown dwarf star.

Yet, as of July 2007, astronomers had identified nearly 250 **extrasolar planets**—or planets outside of the solar system. Astronomers now think that up to 10% of stars like the Sun probably have planets circling them, meaning that there are probably billions of planets in the Milky Way galaxy alone. But, except for a very small handful, none of these planets have actually been seen. So, what's up? How can astronomers know that there are actually planets out there?

"SEEING" OTHER PLANETS

It is too hard to see most planets around other stars, but scientists are convinced they have found them there. How can they be so sure about this? It comes down to their understanding of planetary motion—and in particular, Newton's laws. Here is how they do it.

Position Change

First, Newton's laws say that every object pulls on every other object. The Earth pulls on the Moon, and the Moon pulls back. What this means is that both the Earth and the Moon orbit around a common point, called the center of mass. If someone were watching the Earth closely, even if the Moon were invisible, they would still know that it was there simply by watching the Earth wobble back and forth around the center of mass of the Earth-Moon system.

This effect is not limited to the Earth and the Moon. The Earth pulls on the Sun as well. The problem is that the Earth is so small compared to the Sun that the wobbles are barely detectable. But Jupiter is much more massive; it is a lot easier to see the wobbles from Jupiter pulling on the Sun as it makes an orbit—as long as scientists can make very, very precise measurements of the Sun's position. So, if they are looking for planets around other stars, they just might be able to see the star moving ever so slightly forward and backward—if the planet is big enough to pull on the star. In fact, most of the other planets scientists have found outside the solar system *are* very massive planets (a few times the size of Jupiter); they are not yet about to find smaller planets the size of the Earth through this method.

Redshift and Blueshift Method

In general, a planet's pull is too slight to see visually. If a star is too far away, and if the planet is not large enough, the wobbles may just be too small to notice from Earth. But astronomers can still find planets—sometimes. It turns out that they do not have to actually

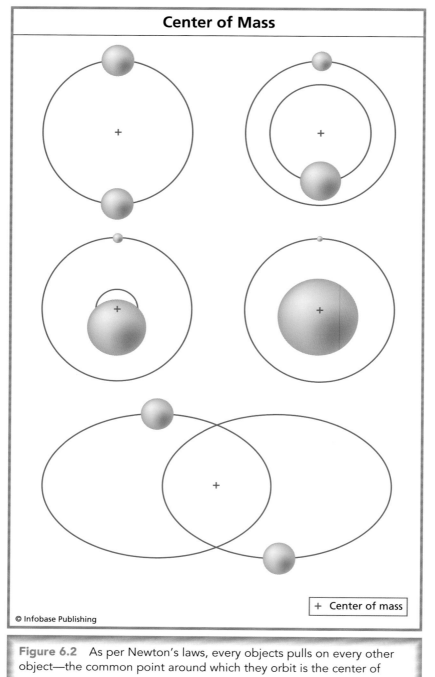

Center of Mass

+ Center of mass

© Infobase Publishing

Figure 6.2 As per Newton's laws, every objects pulls on every other object—the common point around which they orbit is the center of mass.

see the star wobble forward and backward, as long as they can see evidence that it is moving. That evidence is, surprisingly, possible to find—if scientists can measure the star's velocity.

Even if astronomers cannot see a star wobbling, it is still moving. And, in order to wobble forward and backward, the star has to be pulled in one direction and then in the other direction. If scientists are looking for speed changes, then they look to see if the star alternately moves toward and away from the Earth. For example, when a planet is behind a star (from the viewpoint of Earth), it will pull the star away from the Earth, and when the planet is between Earth and the star (in front of the star), it will pull the star toward the Earth. So, when scientists look at the star, sometimes they should see it moving away from the Earth, and sometimes they should see it moving toward the Earth. The problem is how to tell if the star is moving at all, let alone how quickly it is moving. This is where the **redshift** and **blueshift** become important. The important thing to know is that by measuring the redshift and blueshift of light from even a very distant star, scientists can measure changes in the star's speed that are as small as about 1 meter per second—that is only a little more than 2 miles per hour (3.2 kph), or about walking speed. Think about that; from hundreds of light-years away, humans can actually measure a change that is as small as walking speed. *That* is impressive. So, as the planet circles the star, it pulls the star toward and away from it, and astronomers can measure that movement.

Both of these methods depend on measuring the motion of a star as a planet tugs at it this way and that. But the movements and the velocities are so small that it is easy to make a mistake; scientists cannot just take a few measurements and say that they have found a planet—they have to be sure. So, they make these measurements over a long period of time. If they see the same motions over and over again, if those motions are about the same every time, and if those motions are regular (that is, if they happen at the same intervals), then they have found a planet. In some systems, astronomers have even discovered multiple planets.

Of course, the solar system has eight major planets (now that Pluto has been demoted to minor planet status), and four of those planets are large enough to pull on the Sun noticeably. But Jupiter takes nearly 12 years to make a complete orbit, Saturn's "year" is

Redshift and Blueshift

Light can act like a rippling water wave (it acts like a particle, too, but that part is not important for this discussion). The color of the light depends on the distance between the crests of the waves; blue light has small distances between wave crests (short wavelengths), and red light has large distances between wave crests (long wavelengths).

Every atom in the universe gives off light when it is hot enough, and the color of the light that is emitted is different for every element. In fact, every element radiates light with very precise wavelengths, and by measuring its wavelength, it is possible to tell which atomic element (or elements) are present. For example, light with a wavelength of exactly 656.281 nanometers (1 nanometer is 1 millionth of a millimeter)—a specific shade of ultraviolet light—is given off by the hydrogen atom. There is no other element that has this same "fingerprint." This method of identifying atoms in celestial objects works perfectly—until the object emitting the light is moving.

Now, what happens when a shining star is moving toward the Earth? In effect, its light waves become squished together as the star and its light travel toward the Earth—the distance between the wave crests is shorter. This means that the light is closer to blue than the original light was. If the object that gives off the light is moving away from the Earth, the wavelengths will all be shifted toward red. These are called redshift and blueshift. So, redshift and blueshift can reveal if the object shining the light is moving toward or away from the Earth. But they can also reveal exactly how quickly the object radiating the light is moving—by measuring the wavelength with enough precision. With modern scientific instruments, astronomers can measure speeds as low as only a few miles per hour in objects giving off the light. This same effect, called the Doppler effect, can be experienced here on Earth with no instruments other than ears—this effect is why the sound of an approaching

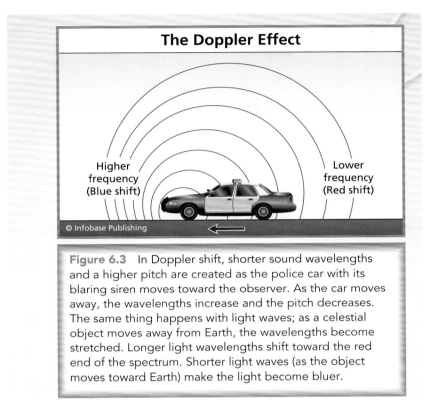

The Doppler Effect

Higher
frequency
(Blue shift)

Lower
frequency
(Red shift)

© Infobase Publishing

Figure 6.3 In Doppler shift, shorter sound wavelengths and a higher pitch are created as the police car with its blaring siren moves toward the observer. As the car moves away, the wavelengths increase and the pitch decreases. The same thing happens with light waves; as a celestial object moves away from Earth, the wavelengths become stretched. Longer light wavelengths shift toward the red end of the spectrum. Shorter light waves (as the object moves toward Earth) make the light become bluer.

police or ambulance siren sounds higher-pitched when the vehicle is approaching and suddenly shifts to sounding lower-pitched as the vehicle passes and begins to move away.

So, when scientists are looking at another planetary system, they can measure the wavelength of the light given off from the star. If the star is being pulled toward the Earth by the gravity of the planet, then the light will be slightly blueshifted, and when the planet is on the other side of the star, the light will be redshifted. So, if the starlight is alternately redshifted and blueshifted, then maybe that means that the star has a companion tugging at it. By measuring the amount of the shift, it is possible to find out whether the companion is light enough to be a planet or so heavy that it must be a star.

almost 30 years long, and Uranus and Neptune take 84 and 166 years respectively to complete an orbit. Someone watching the solar system from a nearby stellar system would need at least 12 years just to realize that Jupiter is there, and it would take nearly 2 centuries to be certain about Neptune. Someone with a lot of patience (and their predecessors and successors), however, would eventually be able to discover all four of these giant planets simply by watching the Sun move back and forth, and toward and away from the Earth.

Other Methods

There are other ways of finding planets as well, but they do not depend as much on Newton's laws. In both of these, astronomers look for changes in the amount of light from the star as the planet moves in front of it. Since stars are much brighter than planets, when a planet moves directly in front of its star, the star looks dimmer.

Figure 6.4 Galaxies can bend light from galaxies behind them, sometimes causing multiple images of the same galaxy—in some cases, there will also be a ring around the galaxy, as with Einstein's rings (*above*). This is an example of gravitational microlensing. Huchra's Lens (*opposite page*) is an image of a distant galaxy that has been bent into four galaxies by the gravitational field of the galaxy in the center.

Unfortunately, many stars are **variable stars**: stars that naturally dim and brighten with time. So, just because a star is sometimes a little dimmer does not mean that it has a planet. Astronomers need to be able to tell the difference between a change in the star and a change due to a planet. This is not always a simple matter, so this method (called the transit method) requires checking and verification by some other means before scientists can say that they have found a planet.

Yet another planet-finding method is called **gravitational microlensing**. A planet or a star will cause space to bend in its vicinity—this bending can actually act as a lens, bending light from behind the planet or star. On a large scale, an entire galaxy or a cluster of galaxies can bend the light from a more distant galaxy. If the alignment is perfect, the light from the galaxy in the background will form a perfect ring, called an **Einstein ring**. Other times, the ring may create multiple images of the same galaxy.

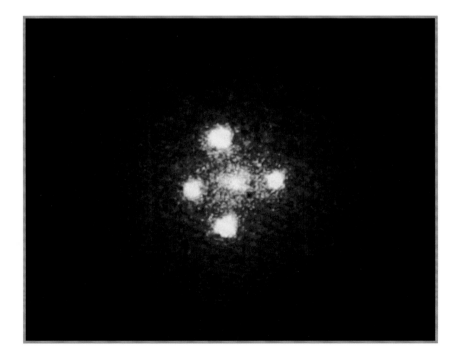

Gravitational microlensing results from similar physics, but on a much smaller scale. In this case, the relatively small gravitational field of a planet can very briefly cause a brightening of the light from the star behind it. So, if a star becomes momentarily brighter, one explanation is that a planet has passed directly between the Earth and the star.

WHAT NOW?

Right now, there are no pictures of most planets outside the solar system. All of the extrasolar planets have been discovered indirectly, so far through the wobbling of a star or some other change. All of the planets scientists have found as of 2008 are far too large to be Earth-like, and they would likely be a poor home for anything that lives on Earth. With only a few exceptions, the first extrasolar planets scientists have found are either far too hot or far too cold for liquid water to exist—and on Earth at least, life needs liquid water in order to form. For the moment, it is unknown what gases are in these planets' atmospheres or if they might have living things of their own. Although most of the first extrasolar planets seem to be "singletons," this is likely due to limited data and observations, and it is likely that they have companions—moons and other planets sharing their system.

Astronomers are already designing telescopes that could directly take pictures of planets around nearby stars. With luck, they will obtain images of several planets within the next several years. Then, scientists can start to look for the sorts of motions that would indicate the presence of other planets in the system—or for evidence that the planets have moons. In fact, it is entirely possible that a gas giant planet could have a habitable moon, but scientists will not know until they can look directly at the gas giant to see if it is wobbling. If so, there will be direct evidence of moons outside our solar system.

A direct image of another planet will reveal clues about its atmosphere. Astronomers have discovered traces of sodium atoms in the atmosphere of one extrasolar planet as it passed directly in front of its star, but sodium will not reveal if a planet has the right conditions for life, or if life forms already exist on it. But if a planet can be seen well enough, scientists can look for water and for oxygen, maybe even for chlorophyll (which could reveal if there are plants like those on Earth).

Finding these things will take time. New telescopes might provide better glimpses of planets beyond the solar system. With luck, in the next few decades scientists will have many more answers.

The Rest of
the Universe

There are four fundamental forces in nature. To understand them better, think of an atom as its own little solar system. Just as the Sun is a huge object that lies at the center of the solar system, an atom has a large core, known as the nucleus, which is larger than any of its other parts. Particles called electrons whiz around the nucleus, just as planets orbit the Sun, although due to a different force.

The strong nuclear force holds together the core of the atom, its nucleus. The weak nuclear force causes particles within the nucleus to transform into new particles that in some cases can escape the atom. But these forces only have any real strength at the core of the atom, or at least over the small distances between particles in the core. The third force, electromagnetism, also affects the electrons orbiting the core of the atoms and can reach pretty far—magnetic fields lace every galaxy—but it is usually too weak to exert much control over distances any larger than several yards (although, in some very rare cases, magnetic fields can control dust and gas over very large distances). Then there is the fourth force, gravity. Inside the atom, it is puny compared to the other three forces. But over long distances, it is the only one out of the four with any real strength. Gravity controls the motions of planets, the shape of a galaxy, and the large groups of galaxies—known as clusters—that reach across hundreds of millions of light-years. Gravity will help to determine the fate of the universe at a time so far in the future as to be nearly impossible to imagine.

Tycho Brahe wanted to describe the universe, but the only universe he knew ended just beyond the Earth. Galileo and Kepler realized that the universe was somewhat larger, and the universe Newton was describing was larger still—almost inconceivably large to an inhabitant of the eighteenth century. For more than a century after Newton's death, the "universe" was the solar system plus a large number of stars that extended to, perhaps, a few tens of thousands of light-years away. Astronomers saw other galaxies, but thought that they resided within the Milky Way. They were thought to be **nebulae**—collections of gas clouds—shaped like spirals. In fact, it was not until the late 1920s and early 1930s that astronomers finally accepted that the universe was huge, and that the spiral nebulae were, in fact, galaxies as large as the Milky Way and millions of light-years away. Today, astronomers recognize that the universe is, in fact billions of light-years in size and that it contains hundreds of billions of galaxies. All of this would have been inconceivable to Newton and those who preceded him, and yet Newton's laws of motion and gravitation describe the motion of objects within those galaxies. Then, Einstein's theory of general relativity provided a description of gravity that can be applied to the motion of clusters of galaxies and the entire universe as a whole. In some cases, the laws of gravity have helped to discover and understand things that still seem strange today.

CLUSTERS OF GALAXIES

Ferdinand Magellan was well into his voyage, and well on his way to becoming the first European to circumnavigate the world. At some point, he realized that the night sky held some "clouds," and that these clouds were apparently fixed in space—they moved no more than the stars themselves. These clouds must lie among the stars, he figured, not in the Earth's atmosphere.[1]

---

[1] Although Magellan is often credited with discovering the Magellanic Clouds, the earliest mention of them dates back to several centuries before Magellan's time—to the year 964, in fact, when they were mentioned by the Persian astronomer Al Sufi.

Today, scientists understand that the Magellanic Clouds are actually small galaxies, like satellites that orbit the Milky Way galaxy. The Milky Way is part of an even larger group of galaxies, called the Local Group—an agglomeration of more than 35 galaxies spread across several million light-years of space.

Tides

Anyone who has been to the sea has seen the tides come in and recede. Twice a day the water reaches a high mark, and twice daily it drops again to a low level. But it turns out that tides affect more than just the Earth's oceans—they are made possible by gravity, and everywhere that gravity works (which is everywhere in the universe), there are tides. Even galaxies have tides—the long tails of the antennae galaxies are streams of stars that have been ripped from the galaxies by tidal forces. What is happening?

Think of the Moon as it travels around the Earth. The Moon is a little more than 2,000 miles (3,219 km) in diameter, so a rock on the far side of the Moon is about 2,000 miles farther away from the Earth than is a rock on the near side of the Moon. So, these two rocks are experiencing different gravitational forces from the Earth.

If the Moon were not there, these rocks would be following different orbits; the nearer rock would be traveling around the Earth more rapidly than the rock on the far side. The rock on the near side of the Moon would be moving faster than it would at the Moon's center, while the rock on the far side would be moving more slowly. If the Moon were not solid, if it were simply a huge collection of rocks, they would all be traveling at different speeds and, over time, the rocks would spread out in space as each one moved at its own speed around the Earth. On the real Moon, these rocks all move at the same speed, held together by the gravity and the strength of the Moon. This means that the

It is possible to determine the motions of each of these galaxies by measuring their redshift and blueshift. These measurements build up a map of where each galaxy is in space and how quickly it is moving. That information, and Newton's laws, can determine how massive each galaxy is. Combining all of this information reveals

rock on the far side of the Moon is traveling faster than if it were freely in orbit, so it is, in effect, being flung away from the center of the Moon, sort of like a ball being swung at the end of a string. This causes a force on the Moon, trying to pull the far half of the Moon away from its center. By similar thinking, the rock on the near side of the Moon is traveling more slowly around the Earth than it "wants" to travel—it, too, is experiencing a force away from the center of the Moon. Rocks are not flexible, so they cannot actually stretch. But it is a different story for water—which is why the Earth's oceans rise as they pass directly beneath the Moon and fall on the opposite side of the Earth.

If a moon gets closer to a planet, these tidal forces grow larger. On the planet, this means higher tides; the forces pulling at the moon grow stronger and stronger. If the moon gets close enough, the tidal forces will eventually be stronger than the moon's gravity and the strength of the rocks. Too close, the moon will simply fall apart due to tidal forces. This distance, the distance at which the tidal forces exceed the forces inside the moon that hold it together, is called the Roche limit, and no large moon can exist closer than this to its home planet.

Something similar happens to galaxies that pass too closely—tidal forces rip out streams of stars from the near and far sides of both galaxies. These make for some of the most dramatic, and some of the most beautiful, pictures in all of astronomy. From thousands of miles to tens of thousands of light-years—tidal forces are the same all over the universe, and Newton's laws explain them all.

that our cluster of galaxies is gravitationally bound—they are all held together by their gravity pulling on each other. In other words, the laws of gravitation shows that our group of galaxies is more than merely a chance grouping of galaxies that just happened to come together for a brief time, like passengers on a train; instead, our small cluster of galaxies is more like a family that lives together for a very long time.

As large as the Local Group is, there are other structures in the universe that are larger yet. The Local Group is part of the Virgo Supercluster, which includes about 100 galactic groups and clusters and extends its grasp over nearly 200 million light-years. As with the Local Group, within our galaxy, and within the solar system, it is possible to understand the motions of each member of the supercluster using laws of physics that were first discovered more than three centuries ago. It turns out that galaxies orbit each other, the same way that planets orbit the Sun.

INTERACTING GALAXIES

Not only do galaxies orbit each other, they also influence each other's motion, and gravity again calls the shots. Galaxies are not only pulled into orbit around one another, they can also tear each other apart.

When gravity pulls on a planet, the planet is a solid chunk of material—it is held together the same way a rock is held together. If gravity pulls on one part of the planet, the whole planet will respond. Galaxies, on the other hand, are not solid; they are more like a swarm of bees flying around their queen. Swinging a board through the swarm (though not recommended!) might push away some of the bees, but what happens to one part of the swarm does not necessarily affect any other parts.

When galaxies approach each other, they start to pull on each other with their gravity. So, the stars in the part of the galaxies that are nearest to each other will start to accelerate toward each other, away from the main body of the galaxy. So, it is common to see a streamer of stars emerging from the near sides of the galaxies. But a stream of stars can also come from the far sides of the

Figure 7.1   Stephan's Quintet is a tight cluster of galaxies that interact due to gravity.

interacting galaxies. These are called tidal tails; they can be seen in the antennae galaxies, two galaxies close enough to push and pull on each other. These galaxies will stretch and squeeze each other, circling around and finally joining together, or merging, after hundreds of millions or billions of years. It is thought that the beautiful shape of spiral galaxies, including the Milky Way, is due to the

The Roche Limit and the Rings of Saturn

Once a moon strays inside the Roche limit, it is only a matter of time before tidal forces tear it apart. As that happens, the rocks that make up the moon start to spread out along the orbit. Eventually, they form a complete ring around the planet, as is likely the case for Saturn and the other outer planets.

Tidal forces can also keep a moon or planet from forming at all. Planets and moons form when gravity pulls materials together. Concentrations of matter have a little higher gravitational pull, so they attract more matter to them. This increases their gravity even more, so they attract still more materials their way. This keeps going until the nearby area has been swept clean. But if the rocks and other raw materials are too close to a planet, if they are inside of the Roche limit, then tidal forces may keep the rocks from ever coalescing into a planet. The gravity of the planet keeps the rocks from ever coming together to form their own planet.

Rings exist in all of the giant planets in our solar system. With the outer planets, scientists cannot be sure if the rings formed from moons being ripped apart or from materials that were prevented from coalescing into a larger objects. Some—in particular, the partial rings around Neptune (called ring arcs)—are probably due to a moon's dismemberment.

collision and merging of smaller galaxies in the distant past. With time, however, the beautiful spirals vanish, too, as spirals merge together into nearly featureless ellipse-shaped blobs.

The same gravitational interactions that form and destroy galaxies can also squeeze clouds of gas and dust. It can be enough to start them collapsing, forming new stars and new planetary systems. When galaxies collide, they cause a lot of disruption—stars almost never collide, but they can be flung off in huge tidal tails that make for some of the most dramatic photos of the universe, and smaller galaxies can even be completely absorbed by larger ones in what is called galactic cannibalism. However, stellar incubators—birthplaces of stars—can also be found in the spiral arms and tidal tails of interacting galaxies.

DARK MATTER

Kepler showed that, in the solar system, the outermost planets move much more slowly than those in the inner solar system. As planets orbit farther and farther from the Sun, they move slower and slower. Similarly, in a galaxy stretching over tens of thousands of light-years, the stars that are far from the center should be moving much more slowly, and those near the galactic rim should be moving most slowly of all. This is what the law of universal gravitation says.

In many galaxies, the stars in the middle form a nearly spherical bulge, and the outermost stars form a disk that rotates around this bulge. In the middle of the last century, astronomers started measuring the speeds of these outlying stars as they orbited their galaxies. By measuring the speeds of these stars, the astronomers could tell exactly how quickly the galaxies' disks were rotating. All of the science was well understood, and everything had been done before, although in other settings.

But when the data were collected and analyzed, the astronomers were shocked. Where they expected to see the stars slowing steadily as they moved farther from the core of the galaxy, instead they saw the speeds level off; for some reason, the stars were not slowing down as they got farther from the middle of the galaxy. What was

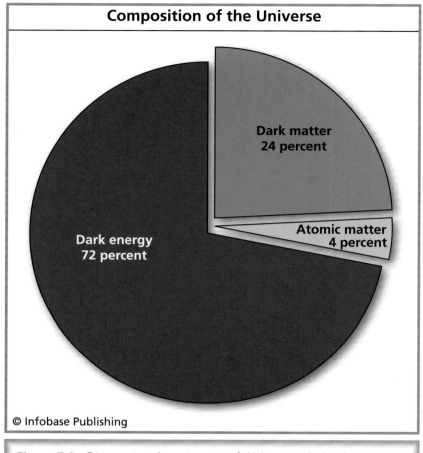

Composition of the Universe

Dark matter
24 percent

Atomic matter
4 percent

Dark energy
72 percent

© Infobase Publishing

Figure 7.2   Discovering the existence of dark matter helped scientists explain how galaxies could rotate the way they do.

happening? Was the law of universal gravitation not universal after all? Or was something else going on?

Astronomers had good reason to believe in the laws of gravity; they were convinced that it must be something else. After years of research, astronomers finally concluded that what seemed ridiculous was actually somewhat less ridiculous than any of the other possibilities. The only thing that made sense was that the galaxies must be surrounded by something that they could not see—something that they could not detect at all, except by its gravity. This invisible matter (now called **dark matter**) added enough mass to the galaxies that the outer stars could rotate much more rapidly than could be explained by the visible matter alone. In fact, when their calculations were completed, it turned out that the matter that scientists can see accounts for only about 10% of all the matter in the universe—90% of the universe is invisible.

This was a shock to most astronomers—except for an astronomer named Fritz Zwicky. Zwicky had predicted just such a thing years earlier by watching the movements of galaxies within galactic clusters. Not only does dark matter affect the motions of stars within a galaxy, but entire clusters of galaxies are embedded in dark matter in the same way that raisins are embedded in raisin bread.

THE FATE OF THE UNIVERSE

Will the universe end with a bang, or with a whimper?

The universe began with a big bang about 13.7 billion years ago. The largest release of energy in the history of the cosmos, the big bang set in motion the expansion of the universe that continues to this day. Beyond our own cluster and supercluster of galaxies, everything in the universe is rushing away from us (and away from everything else in the universe), and the speeds only grow greater for ever-more distant objects. It is not that the big bang flung all of the galaxies outward, it is that the big bang set the entire universe to expanding, dragging the galaxies with it. In essence, the universe is expanding like a balloon that is being blown up, and the galaxies are like dots on the surface of the balloon. As the balloon expands, the dots grow farther apart, their motion driven by the expansion of the balloon. In almost exactly the same manner, galaxies are being pulled apart by the expansion of space itself. The question is whether this expansion will continue forever, or whether something will pull the universe back together again in a "big crunch" at the end of time.

It all comes down to gravity again, and to the behavior of gravity. Think of rolling a ball up a hill. Pushing the ball sends it toward the top, and gravity pulls it back down. Push it hard enough, and the ball will roll over the top of the hill and keep rolling; if not, gravity wins and the ball rolls back down to the bottom. In just the same way, the entire universe was given a push with the big bang. If there is enough matter in the universe (both visible matter and dark matter), astronomers reasoned, then the universe would eventually grind to a halt, and it would start to fall back together some billions of years from now. Some billions of years after that, everything would crunch back together again, maybe launching a new universe in the process. If there is too little mass, if gravity's pull is too weak, the universe would expand forever, eventually growing cold and dark as the last of the stars dies tens of billions of years from now. Scientists thought they would have to weigh the universe to know its fate.

As it turns out, there is something even more surprising at work, and it seems to have given an answer, even though scientists do not yet know how much the universe weighs. It seems that the universe will keep expanding forever, but the reason why is even more unexpected. It turns out that the universe is not only expanding, but that the expansion is speeding up with time. It is as if a ball pushed uphill kept rolling faster and faster. Very odd, indeed.

What astronomers have finally concluded is that, as much dark matter as the universe contains, it contains something even more mysterious; they call this **dark energy**. Dark energy seems to be pushing the universe apart, and its effects seem to be growing stronger with time. Right now, astronomers are not quite sure what this all means or if the dark energy will continue growing stronger into the far distant future. They do not even know what dark energy is, let along how it works. That will, with luck, be discovered with further study—maybe you will be one of the next pioneers of the universe. The explanations to these mysterious new discoveries promise to be surprising and amazing.

LAST THOUGHTS

This last point is important, because it keeps coming up through this whole story. The ancient civilizations looked to the skies and saw their gods. What people eventually found were not gods but, instead, laws of physics that govern the planets and the entire universe. There is no reason why the laws of physics that apply on Earth should work throughout the universe, but they do. That is perhaps the most amazing thing of all—learning that the laws of physics on Earth, and in the solar system, explain events that are happening in the far reaches of the universe. Every new discovery helps scientists understand the universe a little bit better. And every time, humanity finds there is still more to learn.

Glossary

Asteroid A rocky object, too small to be a planet, that orbits the Sun.

Astronomer A scientist who studies the stars, planets, and other bodies outside the Earth.

Axis An imaginary line around which a planet or moon rotates.

Blueshift A change to a bluer color in the light radiated by an object as it moves toward the Earth.

Celestial mechanics A branch of mathematics that describes the motion of planets, stars, and other bodies in the sky.

Center of mass A common point between two objects such as the Earth and Moon around which the objects orbit.

Comet An icy, rocky body that orbits the Sun and usually has a visible tail.

Copernican system A model of the universe that places the Sun at the center.

Cosmology The study of the universe and its origins.

Dark energy A proposed source of invisible energy that is speeding up the expansion of the universe.

Dark matter Invisible material that helps hold the galaxies and clusters of galaxies together.

Eclipse The shadow that is caused when one object, such as the Moon, blocks another object, such as the Sun.

Einstein ring A ring caused by the bending of light around a massive object such as a galaxy or black hole.

Electromagnetism A force that acts on objects through electric and magnetic fields.

Ellipse A shape, resembling a stretched-out circle, that a planet traces out when it orbits the Sun.

Epicycle A small circle inside a large circle; used by the ancient Greeks in their attempts to explain the complex motions of other planets.

Extrasolar planet A planet outside the solar system.

Force Something that pushes or pulls on an object.

Gas giant The name for the outer planets—Jupiter, Saturn, Uranus, and Neptune—which are made mainly of gas.

Gravitational mass A quantity that describes how much force an object experiences from another object's gravity.

Gravitational microlensing A bending of space by any massive object that can focus light from a star and momentarily brighten it, revealing the presence of a massive object such as a planet.

Gravity A force that causes two objects with mass to attract each other.

Inertial mass A quantity that describes how much an object will accelerate in response to a fixed force.

Inverse square law A law that says that the force between two objects drops by an amount inversely proportional to the square of the distance between them, so that objects that become twice as far apart from each other reduce their force to ¼ of the original amount.

Kepler's first law A law that states that planets move in an orbit shaped like an ellipse (flattened circle), with the Sun at a special point called a focus inside the ellipse.

Kepler's second law A law that states that planets travel faster when closer to the Sun and slow down when farther from the Sun.

Kepler's third law A law that allows scientists to determine any planet's distance from the Sun or the length of its year by comparing these quantities to the known distance and length of year of another planet.

Law of universal gravitation   A law that can calculate the force of gravity between any two objects.

Local Group of galaxies   A group of more than 35 galaxies, including the Milky Way, held together by gravity.

Mass   The amount of matter in an object.

Meteor   A small rocky object in the solar system that can create streaks in the night sky when it enters the Earth's atmosphere.

Nebula (nebulae, plural)   A cloud of gas that can eventually form stars and planets.

Newton's first law   A law that states that nothing changes its speed or its direction unless it is pulled or pushed.

Newton's second law   A law that states that pushing something speeds it up.

Newton's third law   A law that states that exerting a force on an object causes the object to exert an equal and opposite force.

Oort cloud   An outer region of the solar system, 50 to 50,000 times the distance between the Earth and the Sun, containing comets and other debris.

Orbit   The path of an object such as a planet or moon around another object, such as a star or planet.

Physical constants   Quantities that define important properties in the universe, such as the strength of gravity and the speed of light.

Planet   An object that orbits a star, is massive enough to make itself round by its own gravity, and does not have comparably sized bodies in its orbit.

Ptolemaic universe   A model of the universe that places the Earth at the center.

Redshift   A change to a redder color in the light radiated by an object as it moves away from the Earth.

Retrograde motion   The periodic appearance of planets moving backward in their paths; this appearance is attributed to the different times it takes for planets to orbit the Sun relative to Earth's orbit.

Solar system   The region of space containing the Sun and everything that it attracts, including the planets, moons, comets, and asteroids.

Solar wind   Streams of particles regularly released by the Sun.

Terrestrial planet   The name for the four inner planets of the solar system—Mercury, Venus, Earth, and Mars—which have rocky surfaces.

Variable stars   Stars that naturally dim and brighten with time.

Bibliography

Aveni, Anthony. *Ancient Astronomers (Exploring the Ancient World)*. Washington, DC: Smithsonian, 1995.

———. *Empires of Time: Calendars, Clocks, and Culture*. Boulder: University Press of Colorado, 2002.

Beatty, J. Kelly, Carolyn Collins Petersen, and Andrew Chaikin, eds. *The New Solar System*. London: Cambridge University Press, 1998.

Calder, Nigel. *Einstein's Universe*. New York: Gramercy, 1988.

Casoli, Fabienne, and Therese Encrenaz. *The New Worlds: Extrasolar Planets*. New York: Springer, 2007.

Ferguson, Kitty. *Tycho and Kepler*. New York: Walker and Company, 2002.

Gleick, James. *Isaac Newton*. New York: Vintage, 2004.

Peterson, Ivars. *Newton's Clock: Chaos in the Solar System*. New York: W.H. Freeman & Company, 1995.

Sagan, Carl. *Cosmos*. New York: Random House, 2002.

Further Resources

Aguilar, David. *Planets, Stars, and Galaxies: A Visual Encyclopedia of Our Universe.* Washington, DC: National Geographic Children's Books, 2007.

de Grasse Tyson, Neil. *The Pluto Files.* New York: W.W. Norton, 2009.

Gingerich, Owen, and James MacLachlan. *Nicolaus Copernicus: Making the Earth a Planet.* New York: Oxford University Press USA, 2005.

Gow, Mary. *Johannes Kepler: Discovering the Laws of Planetary Motion.* Berkeley Heights, N.J.: Enslow Publishers, 2003.

Marvel, Kevin. *Astronomy Made Simple.* New York: Broadway Books, 2004.

Miller, Ron. *Extrasolar Planets.* Minneapolis, Minn.: 21st Century Books, 2002.

Odenwald, S.F. *Back to the Astronomy Café: More Questions and Answers About the Cosmos from "Ask the Astronomer."* Jackson, Tenn.: Westview, 2003.

Spence, Pam. *The Universe Revealed.* New York: HarperCollins Publishers, 2001.

Web Sites

The 8 Planets: A Multimedia Tour of the Solar System
http://www.eightplanets.org
> *Provides a wealth of information on the planets and their moons, with lots of NASA photos, movies, sounds, and links to additional information.*

HowStuffWorks: How Gravity Works
http://science.howstuffworks.com/question232.htm
> *Summarizes what gravity is, provides some basic equations and numbers, and explains the difference between Newtonian and Einsteinian gravity.*

Jet Propulsion Laboratory: A Gravity Assist Mechanical Simulator
http://www2.jpl.nasa.gov/basics/grav/primer.html
> *Explains with video and graphics how using the gravity of planets enables spacecraft to reach their destinations faster and also rescue satellites not in their proper orbits.*

KidsAstronomy.com
http://www.kidsastronomy.com
> *Covers the solar system, civilian space travel, and the size of the universe, and contains astronomy news, a dictionary, games, and activities.*

NASA's Imagine the Universe
http://imagine.gsfc.nasa.gov/docs/homepage.html
> *Designed for ages 14 and up and includes NASA news as well as online exhibits and profiles of scientists.*

NASA: Solar System Exploration
http://solarsystem.nasa.gov
> *NASA's Web site on the solar system, with links to planets, asteroids, comets, and other objects in the Sun's orbit; explains NASA's missions in the solar system and contains articles about NASA scientists and a special section on the science and technology behind solar system exploration.*

Picture Credits

Index

Page numbers in italics indicate images.

About the Authors

P. Andrew Karam is a scientist, writer, and educator who has devoted himself since 1981 to radiation safety. He received his Ph.D. in environmental sciences from Ohio State University. He has written more than 100 technical articles and editorials in scientific and technical journals and newsletters. He has also authored more than 200 encyclopedia articles and several books, including *Rig Ship for Ultra Quiet*, which describes his first encounters with radiation science as a navy technician on a nuclear submarine. He lives in Rochester, New York, with his wife, four children, and too many pets.

Ben P. Stein has been a professional science writer since 1992. He earned his bachelor's degree with honors at the State University of New York at Binghamton. He then attended journalism school at New York University, where he embarked upon a career in science writing. He worked at the American Institute of Physics for 16 years. His writing has appeared in *Encyclopedia Britannica*, *Popular Science*, *New Scientist*, *Salon*, and many other publications. He lives with his wife, son, and two stepsons.